The Bible and Gender

An Exposition of Selected Scriptures

ICOC Teachers Service Team

ILLUMINATION
PUBLISHERS

The Bible and Gender
An Exposition of Selected Scriptures

Printed in the United States of America
ISBN: 978-1-948450-98-0.

Unless otherwise indicated, all Scripture references are from the *Holy Bible*, New International Version, copyright 1973, 1978, 1984 by the International Bible Society. Used by permission of Zondervan Bible Publishers.

Illumination Publishers titles may be purchased in bulk for classroom instruction, teaching seminars, or sales promotional use. For information, please email paul.ipibooks@me.com.

Illumination Publishers cares deeply about using renewable resources and uses recycled paper whenever possible.

Book interior layout: Toney C. Mulhollan.

Cover design: Roy Appalsamy.

ICOC Teachers Service Team

James Becknell	Suzette Lewis
Courtney Bailey	Dr. Gregg Marutzky
Dr. Glenn Giles	Kay Summers McKean
Joey Harris	Dr. Rolan Monje
Tammy Fleming	Dr. Brian Perkins
Dr. Steve Kinnard	Jeanie Shaw
Valdur Koha	

www.ipibooks.com
6010 Pinecreek Ridge Court
Spring, Texas 77379-2513, USA

CONTENTS

Preface

This collection of papers on "The Bible and Gender" was not pulled from thin air; rather, it represents many hours of research, discussion, writing, and editing. This project took approximately two years to complete. The following is a brief overview of our process.

Purpose

In the fall of 2018, the ICOC Teachers Service Team assembled a task force to research biblical passages that speak to the subject of men and women in the Bible. We considered the relationships of men and women to God, each other, marriage, and ministry. The results of this research yielded a group of papers we entitled "The Bible and Gender."

Originally, this project was entitled "A Paper on the Woman's Role." As the project evolved, it became evident that the product from this project was not going to be one paper, but several papers (nine in total). Also, it became evident to the members of the task force that the discussion was not about the woman's role in marriage and the church, but it was a discussion of women and men in the image of God, marriage, ministry, culture, and biblical interpretation.

The task force was a global team of twelve teachers who volunteered their time for this project. The task force was diverse in gender and ethnicity. The task force sought to provide scholarly, exegetical articles that target an audience who desire the "meat" of the Word. Therefore, the papers were based on the Hebrew or Greek text of the passage being considered, as reflected in the papers.

It was not the goal of the task force to comment on how the concepts discussed in the papers were to be implemented on a practical level in local ministries. Neither was it the goal of the task force to provide guidelines for local ministries concerning this topic. The goal was to provide research papers that could be used to facilitate discussions within local ministries concerning the Bible and gender. All but one of the articles include reflections that can be used to help facilitate discussions within churches.

Community Teaching/Community Theology

These articles reflect the process of "community teaching" or "community theology." In many ways, this methodology was the North Star of the task force, driving their process of research and writing. Each member of the task force played a part in shaping each paper throughout the project. Although the voice of the original author or authors remains in the papers, the papers represent the ideas, critiques, criticism, and revision of the entire task force—the result of community theology.

Throughout this collaborative writing, any member of the team could voice her or his opinion during the process. No one voice ruled the day. Before the papers were released, there was one final edit where every paper was reviewed and every member of the team agreed that the final draft of the papers was ready to be released.

As stated, the personal characteristics of the initial authors of the papers (style, outline, flow, syntax) were left intact. Therefore, each paper maintains the personal "feel" of the main author.

Step by Step Process

Step One: The task force decided which passages needed to be exegeted, resulting in nine passages that spoke directly to the topic. Certainly, other passages could have been considered, but the nine passages researched in these papers either provide foundational ideas that must be contemplated or prompt questions that seek answers.

Step Two: After deciding which passages to exegete, the task force assigned various teachers to do the main research on specific passages. Those individuals did the initial research on a passage and wrote a beginning draft of the findings. Each author read the paper to the task force, and the task force commented on the paper. The task force asked the author to make edits on the paper. At times, a second or third teacher joined the original author to add their perspective and/or expertise to the paper. The first author listed on a paper was the lead author/researcher. Names that follow the first author's name joined the paper as collaborators.

Step Three: After the initial drafts were edited, they were reviewed by the task force a second time. More edits followed this review which resulted in the fully edited collection of the papers on "The Bible and Gender."

Step Four: January 2020. The papers were sent to the members of the Teachers Service Team for their comments and feedback. This feedback was considered by the task force and changes in the papers were made based on the feedback. This resulted in draft two of the collection of papers.

Step Five: February 2020. The papers were sent to the members of the ICOC Catalyst Team and the Elders Service Team for their comments and feedback. Their feedback was considered and changes were made, resulting in the third draft.

Step Six: March 2020. The papers were sent to the regional chairs for their comments and feedback. Their feedback was considered. This resulted in draft four.

Step Seven: March 2020. After one last review and edit, the papers were distributed to our ICOC churches. This resulted in the fifth and final draft, the book you are now reading.

The Teachers Task Force on *The Bible and Gender* prays that this book will facilitate discussions concerning this important topic across churches around the globe.

—May 2020

Introduction

God loves humanity. God loves humanity with an unquenchable and ceaseless love. The ultimate expression of his love for humanity was in sending his son Jesus into the world to demonstrate God's love through Jesus' ministry, death, and resurrection. God's love was also expressed in the movement of the Holy Spirit on the hearts of humans to direct them to record Scripture for the edification and instruction of humanity.

God's wisdom is without limit; and in his wisdom, he created humans both female and male. Gender is a God thing.

There are times when gender and Scripture bump up against each other in particular passages that speak specifically to the topic of gender and ministry. This occurs very early in Scripture when God creates humans in his image as both male and female (Genesis 2 and 3).

There are passages of Scripture that mention gender that are difficult to understand. What do we do with passages that state that women ought to remain silent in the church and another passage that speaks of women praying and prophesying in the assembly? What do we do with a passage where Paul says that he does not permit a woman to teach a man and another passage where Priscilla and her husband, Aquila, teach Apollos the way of Jesus more accurately?

Plus, there is a battle in the evangelical world between scholars who hold opposite views on women and their roles in ministry and leadership. Ben Witherington III writes, "In reading through the ever-growing literature dealing with women in the Bible, one is constantly confronted with able scholars who nonetheless come to the text with a specific agenda in mind, whether patriarchal or feminist. This is not surprising in view of the importance of the issue, but when the Bible is used to justify positions which are polar opposites one suspects that something has gone awry" (Ben Witherington III, *Women in Earliest Christianity*, p. 1). Something has gone awry. And since we live in the church as female and male, it serves us as Christians to see what God is saying to women and men in the Bible about gender, roles, leadership, and ministry.

The goal of this collection of articles is to exegete specific passages that speak to the vision God has for women and men in his church. At times, these passages are more specific to women, and at other times, the passages are more specific to men. Often, whether indirectly or directly, the roles of women and men are mentioned in the same passage. Also, we need to realize that all the passages that focus on women in the church were written by men. That's the nature of the text of the Bible.

In the following work, the authors explore the text by using a historical-critical exegetical method of interpretation. This is also known as inductive Bible study. Be aware that reading these papers is not "lite" reading. Many of the authors began by exploring the text in its original language, either Hebrew or Greek. They considered the cultural background and occasional setting that led to the text being written. Only after looking at the text critically to see what the author meant to say to his audience and what the original listeners (or readers) would have understood from the text, did the authors move on to discuss what the text may or may not mean to us today.

This discussion is text driven. We claim to be a people of the Book. If that is the case, then our discussion on gender in the church must be a Bible-based discussion. It ought not to be a 21st-century culture-driven discussion. We begin with the text and then apply the text to culture.

Christianity is a global movement. Culture changes as we move from country to country. The goal of Bible study is to derive meaning from the text and apply it to the culture where we live. It is not to study our given culture and make the text fit into that culture. We need to be students of the text and of culture. But the text should inform our culture. So we start with text; we "trust the text."

Our first paper will look at the creation account in an attempt to set the framework of how God looks at gender. Other papers look specifically at the writings of the Apostle Paul to see what he had to say about women and men in both marriage and in ministry. Also, a passage from the pen of the Apostle Peter will be considered on the topic of marriage.

The goal of all these papers is to help students/readers of God's word interpret passages that speak to the role of women in the ministry of the church. Not every passage on women will be treated here. That wider study lies outside the scope of this collection of articles.

The purpose of these writings is not to define orthodoxy (doctrine) or orthopraxy (practice) for the church. The Bible, not a group of teachers, decides the doctrine and practice of the church. It is the role of the teachers to help explain the meaning of Scripture. We hope this collection of studies offer help in interpreting some difficult passages of Scripture on the role of gender, leadership, and ministry for the glory of God and for the good of the life and ministry of the church.

Conclusion

This book is offered to you in an attempt to create dialogue and to advance the kingdom of God on the earth.

CHAPTER ONE

Genesis 1–3

Joey Harris
Dr. Rolan Monje

Abstract

Genesis 1–3 is the foundation for later exegesis and application for writers in the New Testament along with modern writers considering gender relations in general as well as within the Church. This chapter considers the major interpretational considerations relevant to gender role discussions and evaluates the most likely interpretations relevant to the exegetical, hermeneutical, and practical purposes of this paper.

Introduction

It is hard to overestimate the importance of Genesis 1–3. These chapters of primeval history provide the overture for many vital biblical themes, including gender and gender roles. From these theologically fertile chapters, three important passages of Scripture will be discussed and analyzed:

Genesis 1:26–28	**Creation of Humankind (first description)**
Genesis 2:7–25	**Creation of Humankind (second description)**
Genesis 3:1–24	**Fall of Humankind**

Genesis Chapter 1:26–28

Gen. 1:26— *Then God said, "Let us make mankind in our image, in our likeness, so that they may rule over the fish in the sea and the birds in the sky, over the livestock and all the wild animals, and over all the creatures that move along the ground."*

Gen. 1:27— *So God created mankind in his own image, in the image of God he created them; male and female he created them.*

Gen. 1:28— *God blessed them and said to them, "Be fruitful and increase in number; fill the earth and subdue it. Rule over the fish in the*

sea and the birds in the sky and over every living creature that moves on
the ground."
•(New International Version, 2011 translation is used throughout the paper).

After creating the heavens and the earth and living creatures in the sea, on the land, and in the air, God creates humanity—male and female—in his own image. Human beings are presented in the text as the pinnacle of all creation, as evidenced by their being created last with the preceding creations becoming more complex with each successive day (Sarna, 1989). Relevant to this climactic creative event, some important observations can be made.

1. Significance of Humanity

Humanity is crafted exceptionally. Humans are specially intended for a unique relationship with God. Further, the specified role of stewardship over all things previously created requires that they are fashioned in a different manner from the other living beings.

So God, in the ultimate phase of creation, proposes to make humanity in his own image (Heb. *tselem*) and likeness (Heb. *demuth*). The discussion of the similarities and differences between the two terms, as well as the full concept of *imago dei,* is beyond the scope of this paper, but the Jewish Targum and most scholars today suggest that together they refer to God creating humankind as his living representative and viceroy with the authority and purpose of caring for all other life and taking care of the earth itself. In relation to God, both terms denote a preeminent role. This determination is made for linguistic and cultural reasons, but also on the basis of the text itself, in which God states his intention that humanity should have dominion over all the earth and over all living things (vv. 26 and 28). Interestingly, the royal language used here for humankind contrasts greatly with Mesopotamian cosmogonies, which typically portray humans as lowly slaves.

2. Image as Dynamic

Genesis 1 indicates that humanity was made "in our [God's] image" (v. 26) and not merely produced from the land as with the rest of the living beings (vv. 24–25). Humans are set on a higher plane as an image of deity. But as a representation of God, humankind is more than just a statue. The idea of deputizing God's creation necessitates a dynamic image (e.g., note the use of *tselem* in Genesis 5:3, 9:6).

Being *imago dei* would constitute moral conscience and intelligent action, among other things necessary to represent the Creator. Living as divine representatives assumes immense responsibility, with understandable expectations. The Torah depicts humans as stewards of nature and not owners (Exodus 19:5; Leviticus 25:23–24). They are to care for and attend to the created realm (Genesis 2:15). So although the nuance of "subdue" (Heb. *kabash*) in verse 28 is "to master," humankind is ultimately accountable to the Creator and true Owner (Berlin, 2004).

Crouch (2010) views the text as signifying that the relationship between God and humanity is analogous to the relationship between a parent and children. Thus, humanity is created in "the spittin' image" of God and carries out God's work of taking care of the world.

3. Gender Terminology

In the execution of the divine decree to create mankind (v. 26), the subject of gender is mentioned for the first time (v. 27). It is in this passage that the two sexes—male and female, designated by Heb. *zakar* and *neqebah*—are introduced in Scripture. Purposefully included in the creation of humankind is the creation of two distinct human genders.

> **Genesis 1:26**
> Then God said, "Let us make mankind [ʾadam] in our image, in our likeness..."
>
> **Genesis 1:27**
> ... male [zakar] and female [neqebah] he created them.

The word used to refer to human beings in verse 26 (usually translated as "man," "mankind," "humankind," or "humanity") is ʾadam (Heb. אדם) and is not used here as a proper name but as a collective noun encompassing human beings as a whole (see Genesis 5:2; Crouch, 2010; Greenwood, 2018; Hess, 1990; Reyburn and Fry, 1998) including both male and female genders (cf "mankind" NIV; "humankind" NET; ἄνθρωπον LXX). As Pierce et al. (2005) point out, "Old Testament Hebrew has no common term for 'humanity' other than ʾadam ." There is no linguistic reason to assume a divine preference for the male gender because of the use of the word `adam., just as there is no divine preference indicated by the common English equivalents "man" or "mankind."

The words for "male and female" (*zakar* and *neqebah*) are basic, normative terms used in the Torah referring to the *binary* nature of gender. In fact, in Hebrew, these two different words are etymologically connected to the human reproductive anatomy (HALOT, נקבה ;זכר). The distinction is vital, since it is organically connected to natural reproduction for humans (Gen. 1:28, 2:20) and animals (7:3, 9), as well as to gender identity (Deut. 22:5).

Verse 27 makes it explicit that the *tselem* (image) includes both male and female genders; God creates humanity as male *and* female in his own likeness and image. In other words, both male and female are together created equally in the image of God. The Hebrew parallelism in the three cola of the verse reinforces this, as shown below.

Colon a: God created mankind	in his (own) image	וַיִּבְרָא אֱלֹהִים ׀ אֶת־הָאָדָם
b: He created them	in the image of God	בְּצַלְמוֹ
c. He created them	male and female	בְּצֶלֶם אֱלֹהִים בָּרָא אֹתוֹ
		זָכָר וּנְקֵבָה בָּרָא אֹתָם:

Sarna (1996) maintains that the designations "image" and "likeness" are "democratized" in Genesis, conveying the fundamental idea of human equality. Rabbinic literature, including Rashi, mentions *demuth* (likeness) as indicative of discernment and understanding. Logically, these faculties include both genders.

4. Gender, Blessing, and Divine Command

The creation of gender is related to the command to be "fruitful and increase in number" (v. 28). Mankind is to propagate itself just like other created life (Genesis 1:22) and is repeatedly told to do so (Genesis 8:17, 9:1, 7). Pointedly, the blessing and command come *after* the verse stating the two differentiated sexes. Male and female complement each other by design in gender-specific roles, and it is in the distinction of gender that humanity ensures its existence. This principle is later consolidated in the fruitful union of Adam and Eve in Genesis 2 (where "they become one flesh") and Genesis 4 (where they have offspring "according to their kind" [Genesis 2]). Implied here also is the notion that human sexuality is a gift from God. This divine gift is related to the blessing upon humanity and the subsequent command to multiply.

Furthermore, male and female *together* are given rule over the earth and over all living things (v. 28). The fact that humanity is differentiated seems to be related to their essential purpose of being God's representative and implements of divine rule. Human beings, male and female, are collectively given authority over life and made guardians and caretakers of the planet.

Finally, observe how the author masterfully weaves the strands of blessing and command (vv. 28–30). Blessing in the Torah is related to the giving of life or the enrichment of life (Genesis 1:22, 28, 9:1–3, 22:17; Deuteronomy 2:7). God creates humanity as male and female and supplies their needs (blessing) in order that his intentions are carried out (command). To fill the earth and subdue it, mankind will have to look to God and depend on God. Thus it is God who both gives the command and provides the necessary means to fulfill the same.

Closing thoughts: Genesis 1

An understanding of what humanity is begins with the idea that we are made in the image of God. Genesis 1 tells us that the human creature exists in male and female genders, creatively distinguished. Both genders are equally and fully created in the image and likeness of God. Also, both genders equally share the responsibility to rule over the earth and all other living things.

Genesis Chapter 2:7–25

Gen. 2:7 *Then the LORD God formed a man from the dust of the ground and breathed into his nostrils the breath of life, and the man became a living being.*

Gen. 2:8 *Now the LORD God had planted a garden in the east, in Eden; and there he put the man he had formed. 9 The LORD God made all kinds of trees grow out of the ground—trees that were pleasing to the eye and good for food. In the middle of the garden were the tree of life and the tree of the knowledge of good and evil.*

Gen. 2:10 *A river watering the garden flowed from Eden; from there* it was separated into four headwaters. [11]The name of the first is the Pishon; it winds through the entire land of Havilah, where there is gold. [12](The gold of that land is good; aromatic resin and onyx are also there.) [13]The name of the second river is the Gihon; it winds through the entire land of Cush. [14]The name of the third river is the Tigris; it runs along the east side of Ashur. And the fourth river is the Euphrates.

Gen. 2:15 *The LORD God took the man and put him in the Garden of Eden to work it and take care of it. [16]And the LORD God commanded the man, "You are free to eat from any tree in the garden; [17]but you must not eat from the tree of the knowledge of good and evil, for when you eat from it you will certainly die."*

Gen. 2:18 *The LORD God said, "It is not good for the man to be alone. I will make a helper suitable for him."*

Gen. 2:19 *Now the LORD God had formed out of the ground all the wild animals and all the birds in the sky. He brought them to the man to see what he would name them; and whatever the man called each living creature, that was its name. [20]So the man gave names to all the livestock, the birds in the sky and all the wild animals. But for Adam no suitable helper was found. [21]So the LORD God caused the man to fall into a deep sleep; and while he was sleeping, he took one of the man's ribs and then closed up the place with flesh. [22]Then the LORD God made a woman from the rib he had taken out of the man, and he brought her to the man.*

Gen. 2:23 *The man said, "This is now bone of my bones and flesh of my flesh; she shall be called 'woman,' for she was taken out of man."*

Gen. 2:24 *That is why a man leaves his father and mother and is united to his wife, and they become one flesh.*

Gen. 2:25 *Adam and his wife were both naked, and they felt no shame.*

Genesis 2 retells the events of the first chapter with a focus on the details of how God created human beings. The first three verses are actually the end of the account described in the first chapter. The next account is introduced with 2:4 and continues with a brief description of the state of the earth on the sixth day of creation. Then follows a more detailed recapitulation of the creation of man.

> **Gen 2:7** *Then the LORD God formed a man ['adam] from the dust of the ground ['adam] and breathed into his nostrils the breath of life, and the man ['adam] became a living being.*

God creates a (male) human being, the man, out of the dust of the earth (the word 'adam sounds like the Hebrew word for dirt, clay, ground, 'adamah [Pierce et al., 2005]). The implied imagery of the Hebrew is that God forms the man with his own hands as a sculptor or potter would and then, once satisfied with the form, breathes the breath of life into it, thus creating a living being.

God places the man in a garden that he himself has planted (Genesis 2:8, 15). The garden contains trees that would be aesthetically pleasing and nourishing to the man. The text notes that the center of the garden contained the tree of life and the tree of the knowledge of good and evil. God told the man that he could eat from any tree in the garden but prohibited him from eating from the tree of the knowledge of good and evil (2:16–17). Pierce et al. (2005) note that the woman was not given this command at this point since she did not yet exist.

Several terms employed in the passage deserve some attention, as these will inform biblical exegesis. It is important to note how these lexemes are used in Genesis 2 as well as the rest of the Old Testament.

1. The term 'adam

> **Gen. 2:15** *The LORD God took the man ['adam] and put him in the Garden of Eden to work it and take care of it.*
>
> **Gen. 2:18** *The LORD God said, "It is not good for the man ['adam] to be alone."*

Whereas in Genesis 1, 'adam meant "humanity," in Genesis 2 it becomes a title or category for a specific human, "the man." Here 'adam is not yet being used as a personal name for an individual. Rather, it merely refers to the first instance of a human being; that is, "the man" is equivalent to "the human" (Hess, 1990).

2. The term `*ezer kenegdo*

God remarks that man is somehow incomplete by himself and requires a suitable helper (Heb. *'ezer kenegdo,* lit., "a helper corresponding to" the man, Pierce et al., 2005).

> **Gen. 2:18** *The LORD God said, "It is not good for the man to be alone. I will make a helper suitable ['ezer kenegdo] for him."*

From the immediate context, one may derive the specific interpretative sense of these Hebrew words. This contextual approach is required to avoid error, especially since contemporary readings of Genesis tend to bring out matters of gender bias or exclusivity.

The word 'ezer is viewed by some to imply an inferior or subordinate status relative to the man. There is nothing in the text to suggest this, however; the word simply means "helper" and is often applied to God as the *helper* of Israel (e.g., Hosea 13:9; Psalm 70:5, 146:5), which carries not the slightest implication that God is subordinate to his people. Likewise, *kenegdo* (from *neged*) has received unnecessary modern-day cultural infusions. Perhaps it is best to understand *neged* here as an entity that is "parallel or abreast" (HALOT, נֶגֶד) as in Genesis 33:12.

> **Gen. 33:12** *Then Esau said, "Let us be on our way; I'll accompany you [le-neg-de-ka]."*

In context, *kenegdo* in Genesis 2 simply denotes "being fitting or suitable." The main idea is correspondence—a good match or counterpart. Therefore, the compound term `*ezer kenegdo* is used not in a subordinate sense but in a complementary sense—the helper is to work alongside Adam and to make humanity complete. OT scholar Raymond C. Ortlund, Jr., notes, "The woman, therefore, is a helper corresponding to the man as his counterpart and equal."[1]

---

1. Raymond C. Ortlund, Jr., "Male-Female Equality and Male Headship," in *Recovering Biblical Manhood and Womanhood,* edited by John Piper and Wayne Grudem (Wheaton, Illinois: Crossway, 2006), 104.

3. The terms *'ish / 'ishah*

> **Gen. 2:22** *Then the LORD God made a woman from the rib he had taken out of the man, and he brought her to the man. 23 The man said, "This is now bone of my bones and flesh of my flesh; she shall be called 'woman,' ['ishah] for she was taken out of man ['ish]."*

God presents to the man all the animals in succession, allowing him to name them (Genesis 2:19–20), perhaps to cause the man to realize how much he needs a helper like himself by demonstrating that no other living thing was suitable for the task (Pierce, 2005; Whitekettle, 2009). This seems to be exactly the case given the man's enthusiastically positive reaction upon seeing the (wo)man (the Hebrew words *'ish / 'ishah* sound similar, as do the words man/woman in English) that God created from the man's own flesh and bone. Note as well that the terms *'ish / 'ishah* are used to refer to Adam and Eve in Genesis 3.

As with *'adam* being inclusive of both genders with a sense of equality, *'ish* and *'ishah* stand together to define humanity. That one is derived from the other does not imply one is greater. Brueggemann (1970) explains how Genesis 2:23 "suggests nothing of the superiority of the male" but demonstrates a covenant relationship "rooted in an oath of solidarity." If anything, it is their being "the same yet distinct" that draws them together in divinely ordained union, as is found in the next verse, Genesis 2:24, where the two become "one flesh."

4. The term *tsela*

> **Gen. 2:21** *So the LORD God caused the man to fall into a deep sleep; and while he was sleeping, he took one of the man's ribs [tsela] and then closed up the place with flesh.*

The word traditionally translated as "rib" in most English translations (Heb. *tsela*) actually means "side" in most of its many other occurrences in the Hebrew Bible (Jacobs, 2007, and several Rabbinical commentators in the Talmud). This same word is used in Exodus to describe a side or flank of the tabernacle.

Ex. 26:20 *For the other side [tsela], the north side of the tabernacle, make twenty frames...*

The biblical imagery portrays God splitting one being into two equal and complementary parts that together function as one complete humanity in a harmoniously unified and interdependent relationship with one another. From one, God made two, and the two are to live as one, complementing and helping one another to fulfill God's purpose(s) for them as his representatives and earthly steward-rulers (Genesis 1). The text overall presents a picture of harmonious unity and interdependent functionality between the man and the woman (v. 24, Batto, 2000).

The chapter ends with the observation that the man and woman were naked and felt no shame, thus hinting at the content of chapter three.

Closing thoughts: Genesis 2

God's observation that it is not good for the man to be alone results in the creation of a "suitable helper." Eve, a fitting counterpart for Adam, is fashioned, not from the earth but from the man's side and is meant to be a gift—the sole creature that corresponds best to him as his companion. From man, woman is derived, though she is an independent creation herself, one who acts alongside him to help fulfill God's purposes for humankind.

Genesis Chapter 3:1-24

[1]Now the serpent was more crafty than any of the wild animals the Lord God had made. He said to the woman, "Did God really say, 'You must not eat from any tree in the garden'?"

[2]The woman said to the serpent, "We may eat fruit from the trees in the garden, [3]but God did say, 'You must not eat fruit from the tree that is in the middle of the garden, and you must not touch it, or you will die.'"

[4]"You will not certainly die," the serpent said to the woman. [5]"For God knows that when you eat from it your eyes will be opened, and you will be like God, knowing good and evil."

[6]When the woman saw that the fruit of the tree was good for food

and pleasing to the eye, and also desirable for gaining wisdom, she took some and ate it. She also gave some to her husband, who was with her, and he ate it. [7]Then the eyes of both of them were opened, and they realized they were naked; so they sewed fig leaves together and made coverings for themselves.

[8]Then the man and his wife heard the sound of the Lord God as he was walking in the garden in the cool of the day, and they hid from the Lord God among the trees of the garden. [9] But the Lord God called to the man, "Where are you?"

[10]He answered, "I heard you in the garden, and I was afraid because I was naked; so I hid."

[11]And he said, "Who told you that you were naked? Have you eaten from the tree that I commanded you not to eat from?"

[12]The man said, "The woman you put here with me—she gave me some fruit from the tree, and I ate it."

[13]Then the Lord God said to the woman, "What is this you have done?"

The woman said, "The serpent deceived me, and I ate."

[14]So the Lord God said to the serpent, "Because you have done this,

"Cursed are you above all livestock
and all wild animals!
You will crawl on your belly
and you will eat dust
all the days of your life.
[15]And I will put enmity
between you and the woman,
and between your offspring and hers;
he will crush your head,
and you will strike his heel."
[16]To the woman he said,
"I will make your pains in childbearing very severe;
with painful labor you will give birth to children.
Your desire will be for your husband,
and he will rule over you."

¹⁷To Adam he said, "Because you listened to your wife and ate fruit
from the tree about which I commanded you, 'You must not eat from it,'

"Cursed is the ground because of you;
through painful toil you will eat food from it
all the days of your life.
¹⁸It will produce thorns and thistles for you,
and you will eat the plants of the field.
¹⁹By the sweat of your brow
you will eat your food
until you return to the ground,
since from it you were taken;
for dust you are
and to dust you will return."

²⁰Adam named his wife Eve, because she would become the mother
of all the living.

²¹The Lord God made garments of skin for Adam and his wife and
clothed them. ²²And the Lord God said, "The man has now become like one
of us, knowing good and evil. He must not be allowed to reach out his hand
and take also from the tree of life and eat, and live forever." ²³So the Lord
God banished him from the Garden of Eden to work the ground from which
he had been taken. ²⁴After he drove the man out, he placed on the east side
of the Garden of Eden cherubim and a flaming sword flashing back and
forth to guard the way to the tree of life.

Chapter 3 explains why the world we experience today is so different
from the world created in Genesis 1–2. Specifically, it describes how the
man and woman went from a happy and harmonious interdependently
equal relationship with one another and with the earth and other living
things to a life characterized by pain, struggle, and relational tensions.

Although the entire chapter is important for context, the most
relevant verse to this paper is Genesis 3:16. Some general observations
will be made, followed by a close examination of the verse.

The chapter opens with the serpent subtly questioning God's
authority, causing doubt and tempting the woman to disobey God's
command not to eat from the tree of the knowledge of good and evil (v.
1). The text is completely silent as to how the woman learned of God's

command, but the careful reader notices that her version is slightly different from the version of the command we know was given to the man, with her version including the addition of *"and you must not touch it"* (v. 2).

The serpent sways the woman to disobey God by eating the fruit of the forbidden tree, and she gives some of the fruit to her husband (who is with her), who also disobeys God by eating the fruit, which has instantaneous consequences (vv. 3–7). Though silent, the man remarkably is not absent. Furthermore, his silence need not imply passivity, as some have contended, but rather consent. They are both guilty (Bergant, 2013; Higgins, 1976).

God confronts the couple, and the man blames the woman, who then blames the serpent while admitting that she was deceived (vv. 8–13). Though both sinned, the woman was deceived, while the man knew exactly what he was doing, as he was the one who first received the command directly from God before the woman was created.

In reverse order, God curses the serpent, pronounces judgment upon the woman, and punishes the man because of his sin by cursing the ground from which he was made (vv. 14–19). Interestingly, the punishments meted out have to do with conflicts—struggles in their relationships with the sources of their origin. Taken from the man, the woman will suffer in her relationship with him; taken from the ground, the man will suffer in his relationship with it (Bergant, 2013).

The man then names his wife "Life" (v. 20, Heb. *chavvah,* Greek, *zoe* in LXX), and the chapter ends with God lovingly clothing the couple and ejecting them from the garden to prevent them from having access to the tree of life, guaranteeing that they will die as promised (vv. 21–24).

With that context in mind, let us briefly examine v. 16:

> **16** *To the woman he said,*
> *"I will make your pains in childbearing very severe;*
> > *with painful labor you will give birth to children.*
> *Your desire will be for your husband,*
> > *and he will rule over you."*

This is a very difficult passage to interpret (Reyburn and Fry, 1998), and there have been many, often conflicting, interpretations offered by commentators (e.g., Beattie, 2014; Busenitz, 1983; Condren, 2016; Foh, 1975; Jacobs, 2007; Lohr, 2011; Novick, 2008; Pierce et al., 2005; Roussouw, 2002; Schmitt, 1998; Vasholz, 1994; Vogels, 1996). Nonetheless, some important comments can help to guide discussions on gender issues.

1. Consequences of Sin

The general consequence of their disobedience appears to be pain and labor in work and pain and labor in childbirth (or perhaps a longer gestational period, if Novick, 2008, is correct). Alter (2004) notes that the Hebrew word *'itsavon* is used for both the man's pain in work and the woman's pain in childbirth, establishing a parallel connection between the two.

It is important to note that the woman (unlike the serpent and the man) is the only party punished *without a curse attached.* The serpent is itself cursed by God, and the ground is cursed because of the man's sin, but the woman simply receives the consequences of her sin without any curse being invoked upon either herself or her environment. This is important because many readers assume that the woman is being cursed, which then automatically casts the consequences of her sin in an unnecessarily negative light. As the author of Proverbs puts it, *"My son, do not make light of the Lord's discipline, and do not lose heart when he rebukes you, because the Lord disciplines the one he loves, and he chastens everyone he accepts as his child"* (Proverbs 3:11–12, LXX).

Fleming (2019) expresses this idea very well when she states that God's disciplining of the woman, "...need not be seen as vindictive in any way on God's part (as many women may read it). Was it not the natural consequence of her free will choice when she acted out of suspicion and mistrust toward God, instead of continuing in trust and obedience? The consequence was that she in fact became like God (something Satan knew would happen, using it in his temptation of her in 3:5; something God was protecting her from, but was not afraid of her experiencing, after all) —she became like God, who certainly has pain in all his childbearing as humanity's Father."

2. On "desire" and "rule"

The second clause, particularly the word traditionally translated as

"desire" (Heb. תְּשׁוּקָה, *tshuqah*), has been the focus of many conflicting interpretations.

> **16b** *Your desire [tshuqah] will be for your husband, and he will rule over you."*

Apart from Genesis 3:16, this somewhat obscure noun is used in the Hebrew Bible only two other times: Genesis 4:7 and Song of Songs 7:10. Lohr (2011) comprehensively reviews the interpretation and usage of *tshuqah* throughout history by the biblical authors, the Targums, and the ancient biblical versions in Greek, Syriac and Ethiopic, as well as rabbinical usage and its use in the Dead Sea Scrolls. Lohr argues persuasively and concludes that, in opposition to the traditional interpretation of *tshuqah* as "desire" (ranging from the traditional sexual desire to a broader "intimacy" or "affection" as in Busenitz, 1986, and Vasholz, 1994, respectively), it should actually be translated as "return" with the text paralleling that of the man so that the man will return to the ground from which he was made and the woman will return (or be drawn to return) to the man from which she was made. Meanwhile, Foh (1975) introduced the now-common view that the woman's *tshuqah* was actually a desire to dominate the relationship, which would in turn cause the man to "master" or "rule over" her, thus setting up a continual power struggle (Vogels, 1996).

The second clause of verse 16 is frequently interpreted to mean that the man or husband will "rule" (Heb. *mashal*) over his wife (e.g., Foh, 1975; Pierce et al, 2005). Mashal holds a wide semantic data set. It is used for both people and God (Genesis 24:2, 45:8, 26; Jud 8:23) and even celestial bodies (Genesis 1:18). In context, it does not denote excessive control or tyranny. Interpreters divide over whether the man/husband ruling over the woman/wife is proscriptive (e.g., Foh, 1975) or instead merely describes how things will generally be as a result of sin (e.g., Pierce et al., 2005; Vogels, 1996). The weight of the biblical evidence regarding the relationship between men and women leans toward a descriptive interpretation of Genesis 3:16b.

All things considered, proper interpretation should consider the immediate context of the passage, the type of the discourse (judgment speech in this case) and the flow of the narrative, being careful *not to* read too much into any specific word. For example, that this is a pronouncement of judgment should prompt us to primarily emphasize the changes from the ideal situation depicted earlier. Those departures constitute punishment. Sin leads to disaffection and alienation, in contrast to the harmony and intimacy in Genesis 1 and 2.

Further, as Busenitz (1986) points out, it seems helpful to pay attention to the built-in structure (possibly akin to poetic parallelism) involved in the discourse. In each of the three punishments the pronouncement is given first, then an explanatory statement or expansion follows.

v. 14

punishment: Cursed are you above all livestock and all wild animals

expansion: You will crawl on your belly and you will eat dust all the days of your life.

v. 15

punishment: And I will put enmity between you and the woman...

expansion: [enmity] between your offspring and hers he will crush your head, and you will strike his heel

v. 16

punishment: I will make your pains in childbearing very severe;

expansion: with painful labor you will give birth to children.

our desire will be for your husband, and he will rule over you.

vv. 17–19

punishment: Cursed is the ground because of you...

expansion:

...through painful toil you will eat food from it all the days of your life.

It will produce thorns and thistles for you,

and you will eat the plants of the field.

By the sweat of your face you shall eat bread, till you return to the ground...

The consequence of sin and the fall for the woman could be described as entrenched hardship in fulfilling the roles given to her earlier, co-stewardship and being a companion in procreation. In the aftermath of the fall, her relationship with her husband will be unequal and difficult.

Closing thoughts: Genesis 3

The tragedy of sin and its concomitant punishment are set in contrast to the preceding narrative on God's marvelous creation and empowerment of humanity. Both man and woman receive serious penalties for their disobedience. Relationally, the created order is ruptured, and human life will be marked by frustration and suffering. Redemption is to be found only in God's love and compassion.

Reflections

The opening chapters of Genesis greatly inform our discussions about humanity and relationships, including gender relations. We have seen that as we carefully review the text using hermeneutical tools, we gain clarity about what the text meant to its original audience. We also derive timeless principles leading to contemporary application. While unpacking terminology, we learn to be comfortable with some of the ambiguity that the original Hebrew text presents us in certain passages. More importantly, closer study and reexamination enable us to let go of personal biases and misappropriated cultural influences. With that in mind, here are some salient points for consideration:

> **Genesis 1:** To be truly human requires understanding what it means to be created in the "image of God." Humankind is blessed to share attributes with the Creator. *Imago dei* is an exciting concept that must be robustly defined, reflected on, and personalized. This includes God's design of distinguished equality: Both male and female genders are equally ordained image-bearers and stewards of the earth.

> **Genesis 2:** God remarked that man needs a companion, "a helper suitable for him." Eve is fashioned, not to be inferior, but as a fitting counterpart for Adam. She is the sole creature

that corresponds best to him. So from man, woman is derived, though she is an independent creation herself, one who acts alongside him to help fulfill God's purposes for mankind.

Genesis 3: The consequences of sin are set in stark contrast to the preceding narrative on God's pristine creation and empowerment of humanity. Both man and woman are tried and found equally guilty. Both receive serious penalties for disobeying God. Sin brings about tension and conflict. Sin results in frustration and suffering, but man and woman must learn to live and love in the context of their God-given roles.

As a book of origins, Genesis continues to speak with authority. Its teachings are meant to effectively orient readers to God's wonderful intentions for humanity. Let us allow its pages to shape, reform, and mature our relationships and our lives. As Jacob Neusner (1991) once wrote, "Genesis told about beginnings so as to point to happy endings, and in reading the book of Genesis Israel could find reason to hope for its future in the certain facts of a long-ago past."

Bibliography

Alter, R. (2004). *The Five books of Moses: A Translation With Commentary.* W.W. Norton & Company.

Batto, B. F. (2000) "The Institution of Marriage in Genesis 2 and in Atrahasis," *Catholic Biblical Quarterly* 62:621–631.

Beattie, D. R. G. (2014) "Genesis 3 Revisited," *Expository Times.* 125:282–283.

Berlin, A., Brettler, M., Fishbane, M.A. Eds. (2004) *The Jewish Study Bible.* Oxford Press. Accordance Electronic Ed., paragraph 353.

Bergant, Diane (2013). *Genesis: In the Beginning.* Collegeville, Minnesota: Liturgical Press.

The Catholic Biblical Quarterly 32:4 (October 1970): 541–542.
Busenitz, I.A. (1986) "Woman's Desire for Man: Genesis 3:16 Reconsidered," *Grace Theological Journal* 7:203–212.

Condren, J.C. (2016) "Toward a Purge of the Battle of the Sexes" and "'Return' for the Original Meaning of Genesis 3:16b" *Journal of the Evangelical Theological Society*, 60:224-247.

Crouch, C.L. (2010) "Genesis 1:26–7 As a Statement of Humanity's Divine Parentage." *Journal of Theological Studies*, 61 (1), 1–15.

Fleming, T. (2019) Private email communication on January 12, 2019. Quoted with permission.

Foh, S. T. (1975). "What is the Woman's Desire?" *Westminster Theological Journal* 37: 376–383.

Greenwood, K.R. Editor. (2018) *Since the Beginning: Interpreting Genesis 1 and 2 through the Ages.* Grand Rapids, Michigan : Baker Academic

Jean Higgins, "The Myth of Eve: The Temptress," *Journal of the American Academy of Religion* 44, no. 4 (1976): 639–47.

Hess, R. S. (1990). "Splitting the Adam: The Usage of ʾĀadām In Genesis I-V1," in *Studies in the Pentateuch.* Leiden, The Netherlands: BRILL

Jacobs, M. R. (2007). *Gender, Power, and Persuasion: The Genesis Narratives and Contemporary Perspectives.* Baker Academic.

Lohr, J. N. (2011) "Sexual Desire? Eve, Genesis 3:16 and TŠWQH," *Journal of Biblical Literature* 130:227–246.

Neusner, Jacob. (1991) *Confronting Creation: How Judaism Reads Genesis.* Eugene, Oregon: Wipf & Stock.

Novick, T. (2008) "Pain and Production in Eden: Some Philological Reflections on Genesis iii 16," *Vetus Testamentum* 58:235–244.

Pierce, R. W., Groothuis, R. M., and Fee, G. D. (2005). *Discovering Biblical Equality: Complementarity Without Hierarchy.* Downers Grove, IL: InterVarsity Press.

Reyburn, W.D., and Fry, E.M. (1998). *A Handbook on Genesis. UBS Handbook Series.* New York: United Bible Societies.

Russouw, T. (2002) "'I Will Greatly Increase Your Toil and Your Pregnancies': Alternative Perspectives on Genesis 3:16," *Old Testament Essays* 15:149–163.

Sarna, N.M. (1989) *Genesis.* The JPS Torah Commentary. Philadelphia: Jewish Publication Society.

Sarna, Nahum (1996) "The Mists of Time: Genesis 1–11." In *Genesis: World of Myths and Patriarchs.* Freyerick, Ada. Ed. New York, NY. NYU Press.

Schmitt, J. J. (1991) "Like Eve, Like Adam: mšl in Gen 3,16," *Biblica* 72:1–22.

Vasholz, R.I. (1994) "'He (?) Will Rule Over You': A Thought on Genesis 3:16," *Presbyterion* 20:51–52.

Vogels, W. (1996) "The Power Struggle between Man and Woman (Gen 3:16b)," *Biblica* 77:197–209.

Westfall, C.L., (2016) *Paul and Gender: Reclaiming the Apostle's Vision for Men and Women in Christ.* Grand Rapids, Michigan: Baker Academic.

CHAPTER TWO

1 Corinthians 11:1-16

By Dr. Gregg Marutzky

Introduction

1 Corinthians 11:1-16 raises several issues regarding the women's role in the church including women praying and prophesying in mixed company, the wearing of a covering by both men and women, male/female relationships relating to authority and submission, relational hierarchy between the Father, Son, men, and women, plus propriety of worship, mutual respect for one another, and finally the importance of love and unity in the body of Christ.

Interpretive Approach

The interpretive approach used in this paper includes a hermeneutic based on Cross Theology since the book begins with a call for unity to resolve the divisions reported by members of Chloe's household to the apostle Paul who had planted the church (1 Corinthians 1:10-11, 18-25). The writer seeks to deal with all the various disunifying issues in the church with a call to cruciform living by imitating the Lord Jesus on the Cross (1 Corinthians 1:18-25).[2] Paul describes his audience in the church as unspiritual, in need of the mind of Christ (1 Corinthians 3:1-4). The Corinthians practiced syncretism through combining "sophia" (wisdom) from Hellenistic philosophy with Christianity and describing the resulting spirituality as *"divine sophia."* Nichols writes, "The problem at Corinth is syncretism, which resulted in a completely 'realized' eschatology."[3] Fee writes, "Apparently they have thought of spirituality mostly in terms of ecstasy and experience, which has led some of them to deny the physical body, on the one hand, and to a sense

---

2. Anthony C. Thiselton writes in *1 Corinthians: A Shorter Exegetical & Pastoral Commentary* pages 26-27 a summary of Paul's concerns and the themes of cross and love in the epistle.

3. David R. Nichols, "The Problem of Two-Level Christianity at Corinth," *Pneuma: The Journal of the Society for Pentecostal Studies* 11, no. 2 (fall 1989): 104.

of 'having arrived,' on the other hand."[4]

Cross Theology is based on the gospel of the death, burial, and resurrection of Jesus Christ defining the nature of God as righteous, faithful, and merciful, respectively (1 Corinthians 15:1-4).[5] The death of Jesus reveals a God of holiness, righteousness and justice who extends righteousness to all people through the death of his one and only Son. The Son of God is crucified on the Cross to fulfill the righteous requirements of justice and holiness. The burial of Christ reveals a God of faithfulness to his covenant fulfilling his promises to creation. The resurrection of Jesus reveals a God of love, mercy, and grace to renew creation from the consequences of sin and separation.[6]

The hermeneutical lens of the Cross reads all Scripture seeing God's righteousness, faithfulness, and mercy. Any reading of Scripture without the lens of theology and an accurate view of God produces an imbalanced understanding. Several interpretive tools will be used to discern God's will from 1 Corinthians 11:1-16 including historical-critical methods and socio-cultural techniques.

Context

The pericope of 1 Corinthians 11:1-16 is a formal gathering set in

---

4. Gordon D. Fee, *The First Epistle to the Corinthians* (Grand Rapids: Eerdmans, 1987), 110.

5. Theology of the Cross produces a theology of God by what the passion of Jesus says about God. In her book, *The Classical Theologia Crucis and Karl Barth's Modern Theology of the Cross,* Rosalene Bradbury reviews the scholarship on *Theologia Crucis* and concludes the theologians land in two camps. One perspective views the Theology of Cross narrowly with either a single theme or narrow set of themes and the other perspective uses the message of the cross as a multivalent theological system. Bradbury writes, "This extended position also holds the theology of the cross to be methodology, a way of doing theology, an instrumental touchstone with which to anchor that thought which is properly Christian and to exclude that which is not." (Bradbury, 2012, pg. 17) I embrace the extended, broader view of the theology of the cross as 1 Corinthians 1:18 records, " For the message of the cross is foolishness to those who are perishing, but to us who are being saved it is the power of God."

6. Gregg L. Marutzky, Doctor of Ministry Project Thesis, Transforming Leadership Model for the Denver Church of Christ, May, 2007, Abilene Christian University, Marutzky describes Paul's adherence to Cross Theology throughout the Corinthian correspondence to solve their issues.

a house church or the public assembly in the first century of Achaea.[7] The next section of 1 Corinthians 11:17-34 describing the Lord's Supper indicates the context of both passages as the church worship setting. When the epistle was written, Corinth was a Roman city of standing due to its location as a major trade route for north and south and east and west. The city boasted of a vibrant civic, social, spiritual, and economic environment due to trade. Corinth attracted patrons of significant long-term family wealth and holdings as well as many artisans and traders who became wealthy in Corinth due to the strong economy.

Therefore Corinth had "old money" and "new money." The healthy economy produced a steady increase in population requiring more civic investment from patronage. The Roman government maintained a strong presence in Corinth due to the importance of the city economically and politically. The church in Corinth struggled with the division between the rich and the poor. For example, the lawsuits between believers addressed in 1 Corinthian 6 demonstrate the fractured relationship between rich and poor in the congregation. Wealthy patrons clashed with Paul over his refusal to accept patronage (1 Corinthians 9:1-19) and the rich who held an inflated view of their own spirituality based on Greco-Roman cultural values abused the poor in the congregation. The wealthy members did not include the poor in their meals on Sunday. Paul addressed this issue in 1 Corinthians 11 by explaining the meaning of the Lord's Supper. The communion meal celebrates the hospitality of God towards all–Jew or Greek, slave or free, rich or poor, male or female. The Lord's Supper is intended to build up the body of Christ, signifying the unity of God's people; it is not intended to foster secular divisions.[8]

The cosmopolitan environment of Corinth fostered the latest trends in the Empire socially, politically, spiritually, and economically. One trend regarding the role of women has been described as the

---

7. Ben Witherington III, *Conflict and Community in Corinth: A Socio-Rhetorical Commentary on 1 and 2 Corinthians* (Grand Rapids: Eerdmans, 1995), describes house church setting, pages 30-32. Also see Winter, Bruce W., *Roman Wives, Roman Widows: The Appearance of the New Women and the Pauline Communities*. Grand Rapids: Eerdmans, 2003, pages 21-31.

8. William F. Orr and James Arthur Walther, *I Corinthians: A New Translation, Anchor Bible* 32 (Garden City, NY: Doubleday, 1976), describes the context of Corinth on pages 269-72.

"New Roman Woman."[9] The dependence of women on men decreased when females were afforded the opportunity to become economically independent. Corinth provided an ideal environment for skilled women to gain significant wealth through importing and exporting goods or becoming skilled as an artisan to sell goods produced by their own expertise.

A feminist movement evolved in the Roman Empire during the Pax Romana that allowed women's voices to be heard and females to gain personal stature socially and economically apart from a father or husband.[10] The culture of Corinth was Greco/Roman as Hellenization undergirded all social activities, but civic life was controlled by the Roman officials.[11]

Roman law and Greek customs have implications on our passage. The context of Corinth is a society with an honor/shame culture and a patron/client economy. Loyalty or faithfulness and gratitude or grace are highly regarded in patron/client cultures while saving face and upholding the honor of the family or group is essential in honor/shame environments. Two significant aspects of the context of the pericope are the societal customs and laws regarding head coverings, plus the feminist movement in the Roman Empire during the first century.

Exegetical Clues

Examination of any pericope requires an understanding of the context including the original audience and setting. The desire of the exegete is to gain an understanding of how the original audience understood the passage. Secondly, it is necessary to allow the passage

9. Ben Witherington III, *Conflict and Community in Corinth: A Socio-Rhetorical Commentary on 1 and 2 Corinthians* (Grand Rapids: Eerdmans, 1995), describes the context of 1 & 2 Corinthians in the introduction, pages 1-34. Also see Winter, Bruce W., *Roman Wives, Roman Widows: The Appearance of the New Women and the Pauline Communities.* Grand Rapids: Eerdmans, 2003. Winter describes the first-century culture regarding women and proposes a feminist movement described as the "New Roman Woman."

10 Winter, Bruce W., *Roman Wives, Roman Widows: The Appearance of the New Women and the Pauline Communities.* Grand Rapids: Eerdmans, 2003, pages 21-31.

11. Ben Witherington III, *Conflict and Community in Corinth: A Socio-Rhetorical Commentary on 1 and 2 Corinthians* (Grand Rapids: Eerdmans, 1995), describes the mixed influence of Hellenization and the Roman Empire, pages 22-30.

to explain itself by understanding the structure and obvious features before addressing the complexities. Other passages that echo themes from the pericope can be used for interpretive insights. Finally, the entire understanding of a passage should be congruent, with no contradictions.

Outstanding features of the Corinthian correspondence and 1 Corinthians 11:1-16 specifically:

1. Paul is responding to questions raised by the community, 1 Corinthians 7:1-10:1.

2. Paul is addressing issues contributing to disunity among the Corinthian disciples, 1 Corinthians 1:11.

3. Paul seeks to persuade the church in Corinth without exerting his authority as an apostle, 1 Corinthians 4:14-17.

4. Some in the Corinthian community are critical or resistant to Paul's leadership, 1 Corinthians 4:18-21.

5. Paul's instructions establish the goals of unity and love within the community, 1 Corinthians 13:1-13.

6. Paul combats spiritual immaturity and insufficient spirituality with instruction on cruxiformity, 1 Corinthians 3:1-23.

7. 1 Corinthians 11 addresses issues of corporate worship including the Lord's Supper, plus women praying and prophesying in mixed company.

8. Women in Corinth were praying and prophesying in the corporate worship, 1 Corinthians 11:5.

9. Some of the women participating in the corporate worship did not cover their heads as was the tradition in the other churches, 1 Corinthians 11:6.

10. Paul exhorts the women in Corinth to cover their heads during corporate worship, 1 Corinthians 11:10.

11. The reasons for covering the heads involved issues of honor and shame, 1 Corinthians 11:4-5.

Key structures in the passage:

Parallelism: Men were required to pray and prophesy with their heads uncovered according to verse 4, *"Every man who prays or prophesies with his head covered dishonors his head."*[12] The opposite is true for women according to verse 5, *"But every woman who prays or prophesies with her head uncovered dishonors her head—it is the same as having her head shaved."* Women must have a covering on their heads to pray and prophesy.

Another parallelism is the contrast between hair length for men and women for glory or shame in verse 14, *"Does not the very nature of things teach you that if a man has long hair, it is a disgrace to him,"* compared to verse 15, *"But that if a woman has long hair, it is her glory? For long hair is given to her as a covering."* Nature produces physical characteristics between men and women displaying an obvious difference between the sexes. Paul includes hair length as one of the physical differences to recognize gender diversity.

Chiasm: A-B-C-D-C-B-A, Pattern teaches us how to worship God honorably as men and women with gender distinctions between males and females due to church traditions, headship, gender distinctions, and creation order. The chiasm culminates with a reference to the propriety of women in respect to divine beings (angels). This chiasm points to the importance of order and propriety in worship.

1. **A – Traditions** (*paradosis*): (Vs. 2) *"I praise you for remembering me in everything and for holding to the traditions just as I passed them on to you."*

2. **B – Headship** (*kaphale*): (Vs. 3) *"But I want you to realize that the head of every man is Christ, and the head of the woman is man, and the head of Christ is God."* Male Covered Head Shameful: (Vs. 4) *"Every man who prays or prophesies with his head covered dishonors his head."* Female Uncovered Head Shameful: (Vs. 5) *"But every woman who prays or prophesies with her head uncovered dishonors her head—it is the same as having her head shaved."* Order & Propriety: (Vs.

12. All references are from NIV, 2010 in this paper unless otherwise noted.

33

6) *"For if a woman does not cover her head, she might as well have her hair cut off; but if it is a disgrace for a woman to have her hair cut off or her head shaved, then she should cover her head."*

3. **C – Male & Female Glory** (*doxa*): (Vs. 7) *"A man ought not to cover his head, since he is the image and glory of God; but woman is the glory of man."* Creation Order: (Vs. 8) *"For man did not come from woman, but woman from man;"* Creation Purpose: (Vs. 9) *"Neither was man created for woman, but woman for man."*

4. **D – Creation Order** (*exousia*): (Vs. 10) *"It is for this reason that a woman ought to have authority (exousia- power) on her own head, because of the angels."*

5. **C – Male & Female Glory** (*doxa*): (Vs. 11) *"Nevertheless, in the Lord woman is not independent of man, nor is man independent of woman."* Order & Propriety: (Vs. 12) *"For as woman came from man, so also man is born of woman. But everything comes from God."*

6. **B – Headship** (*kaphale*): (Vs. 13) *"Judge for yourselves: Is it proper for a woman to pray to God with her head uncovered?"* Male Covered Head Shameful: (Vs. 14) *"Does not the very nature of things teach you that if a man has long hair, it is a disgrace to him."* Female Glory (Vs. 15) *"But that if a woman has long hair, it is her glory? For long hair is given to her as a covering."*

7. **A – Customs** (*sunetheia*): (Vs. 16) *"If anyone wants to be contentious about this, we have no other practice—nor do the churches of God."*

Key arguments in the passage:

1. Paul begins by listing an ordering of relationships with God first, Jesus second, males third, and females fourth according to verse 3 *"But I want you to realize that the head of every man is Christ, and the head of the woman is man, and the head of Christ is God."* He states this proposition as though it is understood and accepted by everyone. The order is not in

sequence from top to bottom and the listing excludes angels. Debate occurs whether the relationship is between a married husband and wife or between all men and women in the fellowship.

2. The apostle's second argument for women covering their heads while praying and prophesying appeals to creation in verse 7, *"A man ought not to cover his head, since he is the image and glory of God; but woman is the glory of man,"* verse 8, *"for man did not come from woman, but woman from man,"* and verse 9, *"neither was man created for woman, but woman for man."* This is a curious argument since the Genesis record describes both the male and female created in the image of God. The woman was taken from the side of man to be "a power equal to" (`ezer) the man since he was lonely without a partner. The argument is founded on created order not image since both male and female are created in the image of God. (Genesis 1:27 – *"So God created mankind in his own image, in the image of God he created them; male and female he created them."*) Genesis records that the female was created from the male, Genesis 2:24 – *"Then the LORD God made a woman from the rib (tsela- side) he had taken out of the man, and he brought her to the man,"* and the female was created for the purpose of partnering with the male, Genesis 2:18 – *"The LORD God said, 'It is not good for the man to be alone. I will make a helper suitable for him.'"* God made the male from the ground while God made the female from the male. God split the man to create the woman. Similarly, God is three the Father, Son, and Holy Spirit. The Father, Son and Holy Spirit are God while the man and woman are both human. The role and order of the Trinity are similar to distinctive roles and order among humans. Both men and women are human but different sexes, male/female.

3. The third argument in the passage regarding the reason women should cover their heads during prayer and prophecy is because of angels in verse 10, *"It is for this reason that a woman ought to have authority on her own head, because of*

the angels. " Angels refers to heavenly beings as well as earthly messengers. The word angels -*ἄγγελος-anggelos* literally means messengers. This verse raises several questions. Could the messengers be the *gynaikonomos* or dress code police of the first century?[13] Was the appeal to angelic beings an addition to the spiritual hierarchy used in verse 3, with angels being inserted above women? As a possible rebuttal to this proposal we could ask, are not angels also above males on earth in the heavenly hierarchy? The reference to angels directs the audience to the spiritual realm. Worship directs our attention to God. A role of angels in heaven is to model reverence in worship of Yahweh by covering themselves with their wings (Isaiah 6:2).[14]

4. The fourth reason for women to cover their heads while praying and prophesying deals with the differentiation between the genders regarding hair length. Paul argues for men to be identified as males by short hair and women are identified by long hair as females. Curiously, Paul writes nature instructs men to have short hair and women long hair. Other than male-pattern baldness this seems unclear in nature. What does Paul mean by nature? Is nature the description revealed in creation?

Important questions about the passage:
1. Why is the covering of women or uncovering of men so significant?
2. Could the problem with the women in Corinth be disorderly conduct?
3. Does this passage teach that women should pray and prophesy in worship?
4. What are the arguments for a covering for women in this pericope?
5. What kind of covering is to be worn in worship? What does a covering have to do with authority?

13. Bruce W. Winter describes the importance of veils for women in Roman Wives, *Roman Widows: The Appearance of the New Women and the Pauline Communities* in chapter 5, pages 77-96. The "gynaikonomos" are described on page 82 of the chapter.
14. Anthony C. Thiselton writes on page 176 in *1 Corinthians: A Shorter Exegetical & Pastoral Commentary* that "angels" are the heavenly host who model reverence in worship by covering themselves with their wings citing Isaiah 6:2.

6. Why should men have short hair and women long hair according to this passage?
7. Why is it a disgrace for men to have long hair and women to have short hair?
8. Why are the angels referenced in this passage?
9. What principles are taught in these scriptures that can be applicable to a different culture and context?
10. Is creation order significant in the roles of men and women?

Exegesis of 1 Corinthians 11:1-16 – Head Covering in Worship:

(Vs. 1) *"Follow my example, as I follow the example of Christ."* This verse is a guiding instruction for the church. Discipleship includes godly imitation of Jesus. This verse is often excluded from an investigation of the women's role in 1 Corinthians 11 but it is included here for purposes of connecting the cruciform theme in 1 Corinthians.[15] Paul calls the disciples in Corinth back to the imitation of Jesus throughout the book. The Corinthians were preoccupied with assimilating to the carnal culture of the city to the neglect of Christ-like virtues. The book deals more with correctives than directives due to pressing issues causing disunity. Paul is answering questions posed to him that were producing division in the church. Paul repeatedly admonishes the Corinthians throughout the letter to stop tearing down one another in the body of Christ but rather build up the church through love and cruciform imitation of Jesus. Paul calls the disciples back to the message of the cross to restore unity.

(Vs. 2) *"I praise you for remembering me in everything and for holding to the traditions just as I passed them on to you."* Paul appeals to the Corinthians throughout the book through his relationship with the disciples and not his office as an apostle. Paul seeks to persuade the Corinthians through reminding them of his example and through their relationship to him as the church planter. The first-century church had traditions and patterns practiced in all the churches. The word traditions, παράδοσις- *paradosis* meant precepts or laws.[16] The traditions might have been Christian

---

15. Lee-Barnewall, 2016, p. 113.
16. Ben Witherington III, *Conflict and Community in Corinth: A Socio-Rhetorical Commentary on 1 and 2 Corinthians* (Grand Rapids: Eerdmans, 1995), describes possible understanding of traditions, pages 231-240.

practices, Jewish ordinances, Hellenistic customs, or Roman laws. The traditions may have been communal covenants for unity and mutual edification in the church or cultural practices that were not in opposition to Christian orthodoxy but maintained peace between the church and society-at-large. A question to ask is which of these possibilities is in play in this case as it may influence our interpretation. Recognizing the patterns in scripture adjusted for context informs us of practices for today. It is fine for the brotherhood to have common practices as long as they are reverent towards God. What traditions are they upholding that he is praising? What practices are irreverent causing Paul to admonish the church? Is Paul about to correct the church for not holding to a custom in the church practiced by the society? Or is the Apostle ironically praising the congregation in advance for the response he desires from his instruction?

(Vs. 3) *"But I want you to realize that the head of every man is Christ, and the head of the woman is man, and the head of Christ is God."* This verse seems to affirm "headship" in the context of worship assemblies of the church since Paul is about to discuss the corporate Lord's Supper. Is Paul defining a spiritual hierarchy of authority for the church? The issue hinges on the definition of the word κεφαλή- *kephale,* which means topmost or head.[17] The predominate definition for kephale is "head" defining a hierarchy with authority and subordination of the parties.[18] A disputed definition that is only found in a very small minority of classical Greek references of *kephale* is "source" allowing for greater equality of the sexes with no authority and submission between men and women.[19] Christ does have authority over humans both males and females as a member of the Godhead or Trinity. When *kephale* is understood as head the pericope is congruent with references to head, hair, and authority regarding

---

17. Ben Witherington III, *Conflict and Community in Corinth: A Socio-Rhetorical Commentary on 1 and 2 Corinthians* (Grand Rapids: Eerdmans, 1995), describes the interpretations of kephale, pages 237-238.
18. Thomas R. Schreiner provides the Complementarian perspective in chapter 5 of *Recovering Biblical Manhood & Womanhood,* pages 124-139. Schreiner argues kephale means head creating hierarchy with authority and submission.
19. Gordon D. Fee provides the egalitarian perspective in chapter 8 of *Discovering Biblical Equality: Complementary Without Hierarchy,* pages 142-160. Fee argues that kephale means source to avoid hierarchy in the passage.

both males and females.[20] Some contemporary interpreters argue that supporting kephale as head has led to the subordination of women and diminishment of female personhood thus negating the identity of women made in the image of God.[21] Headship does not diminish women but rather describes the heavenly hierarchy described in this passage. Adam was formed first and Eve second thus creating a natural hierarchy with Adam as head of Eve.[22] Does authority accompany creation order

---

20. For this reason and what is noted below in this footnote, we have chosen the translation of kephale as "head" for these papers: (1) Although the classical Greek Lexicon, Liddell and Scott (Henry George Liddell and Robert Scott, *A Greek-English Lexicon.* Oxford: Clarendon, 1996) gives a possible definition of "source" among several definitions for kephale, it does not list 1 Corinthians 11 nor Ephesians 5 under this definition. This lexicon is also not a specialty lexicon for biblical (koine) Greek. (2) All the standard koine Greek (the Greek of the Bible) specialty lexicons support the definition for *kephale* here in 1 Corinthians 11 and/or in Ephesians 5 as being a metaphorical use of the term "head": (a) Frederick William Danker and Walter Bauer, (*A Greek-English Lexicon of the New Testament and other Early Christian Literature,* Third Edition (BDAG). Chicago: University of Chicago Press, 2000) translate it here as "superior rank" for 1 Corinthians 11 and Ephesians 5. (b) J. H. Thayer (*The New Greek-English Lexicon of the New Testament,* Peabody, MA: Hendrickson, 1981) lists Ephesians 5 and 1 Corinthians 11 under "Metaph.. anything supreme, chief, prominent; of persons, master, lord: . . . of a husband in relation to his wife . . .of Christ , the lord of the husband . . . of the church". (c) Edward Robinson (*A Greek and English Lexicon of the New Testament* (Boston and New York: Houghton, Mifflin and Company, 1887) lists 1 Cor 11:3 and Eph. 5:23 under the idea of "the head, the chief, one to whom others are subordinate; e.g. a husband in relation to a wife . . . Of Christ in relation to his church, which is his body . . . and its members. . . Of God in relation to Christ, 1 Cor. 11:3". (d) Johannes P. Louw and Eugene A. Nida, (editors of *Greek-English Lexicon of the New Testament Based on Semantic Domains,* second edition. New York, United Bible Societies, 1989) list the definition as "one who is of supreme or pre-eminent status, in view of authority to order or command-'one who is the head of, one who is superior to, one who is supreme over." They then list Ephesians 4:15 here with respect to Christ being the head and then state 'Christ is supreme over every man, the husband is supreme over his wife, and God is supreme over Christ' 1 Cor 11:3." (3) Wayne Grudem, in an exhaustive study of the term *kephale* in ancient Greek, concludes that "there is no linguistic basis for proposing that the New Testament texts which speak of Christ as the head of the church or the husband as head of the wife can rightly be read apart from the attribution of authority to the one designated as 'head'" (*Recovering Biblical Manhood & Womanhood,* pages 467-468).
21. Gordon D. Fee provides the egalitarian perspective in chapter 8 of *Discovering Biblical Equality: Complementary Without Hierarchy,* pages 142-160.
22. Thomas R. Schreiner provides the Complementarian perspective in chapter 5 of *Recovering Biblical Manhood & Womanhood,* pages 124-139. Schreiner begins with kephale as head but allows for the source interpretation to reinforce male hierarchy since males were created first before females, pages 132-134.

or birth order? Even if it does not (as it did not with Jacob and Esau), 1 Corinthians 11 seems to imply that man is the head of woman and that a husband is the head of his wife. Birth order defined privilege and responsibility in the ancient world. Does headship necessitate authority and subordination? Privileges of the first born or primogeniture did not necessarily include authority in the ancient world though it often did.[23]

(Vs. 4) *"Every man who prays or prophesies with his head covered dishonors his head."* Head coverings were signs of propriety in Greco/Roman society.[24] Head coverings were symbols of hierarchy and submission. What does it mean to dishonor the head? The covering defines a subordinate relationship. An understanding of the relationships in the Godhead or Trinity might inform our understanding of headship and authority in Christian relationships. Since in the Godhead the Father (head) is equal to the Son and Spirit with different roles then it follows males and females can be equal with different roles. Also, since the Trinity has an order of Father, Son, and Holy Spirit then the ordering of males and females is plausible. Parsing concepts to distinguish absolute arguments inevitably leads to polarized positions. But allowing dialectic tension to exist allows for a healthy balance and avoidance of extreme thinking. Two concepts can be true at the same time. Birth order seems to allow for mutuality, individuality, uniqueness, mutual respect, differentiation, and relationship. But headship describes spiritual hierarchy, benevolent authority, and servant leadership.

(Vs. 5) *"But every woman who prays or prophesies with her head uncovered dishonors her head—it is the same as having her head shaved."* Females praying and prophesying in the assembly is assumed in this passage.[25] The women of Corinth were praying and prophesying in church. The issue of concern is the uncovering of the head. Praying and prophesying are

23. Michelle Lee-Barnewall writes in *Neither Complementarian nor Egalitarian* that primogeniture was not iron-clad in the ancient world on page 138.
24. Bruce W. Winter describes the importance of veils for women in *Roman Wives, Roman Widows: The Appearance of the New Women and the Pauline Communities* in chapter 5, pages 77-96. Head Coverings are describe on pages 91-93 of the chapter. Also Anthony C. Thiselton writes "a respectable married woman, loyal to her husband would not wish to dispense with her hood or veil in public" on page 21 of *1 Corinthians: A Shorter Exegetical & Pastoral Commentary.*
25. Prophesying in this context is the gift of prophecy referenced in 1 Corinthians 12. A general definition of prophecy is "speaking the inspired word of God." Preaching has been compared to prophesying since the inspired word of God in scripture is used.

audible acts in the assembly in which women participated according to 1 Corinthians 14 (e.g., at least prophecy is for the edification of others). What implications does this verse hold for Christian churches today? Women can pray and prophesy in the church as long as the same qualifications Paul placed on the Corinthian women are respected. The qualifications Paul makes were in a particular context (Corinth) in time (1st Century) but were based on the theological principles of headship, creation, and propriety. The concern of Paul's text seems to be how the women of Corinth were praying and prophesying. What corrective is Paul seeking to initiate? Should women recognize God's authoritative hierarchy while participating in worship? What does that look like? The issue is an uncovered head representing impropriety and irreverence. Paul equates an uncovered head by women in Corinth as an extreme behavior equivalent to shaving their head. A shaved-female head in the ancient world was used to shame the woman. Adulteresses were denoted for the rest of the community by shaving their head.[26] Paul seems to want to challenge the behavior of some of the women in Corinth for uncovering their heads while praying and prophesying. Interestingly, only married women in Greco/Roman society were required to cover their heads in public. An unmarried woman was not required to cover her head but was required to adhere to a particular dress code to avoid public shaming by officials designated to police the propriety exhibited by women. The public dress code enforcers were known as *gynaikonomos*.[27] Therefore it seems reasonable to conclude that Paul is correcting an impropriety of the traditional dress code in Corinth. Dressing or speaking improperly draws attention in any setting that has customary norms. The dress and conduct of some of the sisters in the Corinthian church needed to be addressed to maintain unity in the church. The women's actions could have been considered disorderly if the practice disrupted worship. But was the behavior a violation of Christian orthodoxy or a disruptive practice that violated conscience, not doctrine. A clue is the appeal made

26. Anthony C. Thiselton describes the shame of a shaved head on a woman on pages 172-173 of *1 Corinthians: A Shorter Exegetical & Pastoral Commentary.* He also notes the importance of gender distinction in the wearing of a hood or the length of the hair.
27. Bruce W. Winter describes the role of the *gynaikonomos* in the enforcing of Roman codes in *Roman Wives, Roman Widows: The Appearance of the New Women and the Pauline Communities* in chapter 5, pages 88-90.

to a spiritual hierarchy or order.

(Vs. 6) *"For if a woman does not cover her head, she might as well have her hair cut off; but if it is a disgrace for a woman to have her hair cut off or her head shaved, then she should cover her head."* Paul intensifies his argument against the uncovering of the head by the Corinthian women who were praying and prophesying by equating the action to the public shaming of an adulteress by shaving the head. Paul hyperbolizes the dismissal of wearing a veil or shawl by the worshipping females as dishonorable and as shameful – appearing like an adulteress. Paul rhetorically asks whether a woman should cover her head and the answer he gives is a resounding, yes! Yes, her head should be covered in the Corinthian church since it is a disgrace (αἴσχρον- *aischron* - shameful) in their cultural context. Who is being shamed? Is she shaming herself for not acting feminine like a woman or is she shaming her husband? Is the shame a lack of gender distinction between male and female or is the disgrace due to usurping her husband's authority? Is the impropriety shameful towards the ultimate head- God? Would Paul publicly correct the praying and prophesying women of Corinth for a dress-code violation? Gender distinction was also described in Greco/Roman society by different uses of a "veil." A shoal or Roman toga was pulled up over the head during the act of praying or prophesying.[28] Later in the passage we will see God honors/recognizes women through long hair.

(Vs. 7) *"A man ought not to cover his head, since he is the image and glory of God; but woman is the glory of man."* Gender distinction is rooted in God's act of creation. Creation order defines worship decorum. This verse is somewhat difficult to reconcile as noted above with the Genesis account of the male and female both being created in the image of God, Genesis 1:27. The birth order of the male and female is recorded in Genesis 2. God created the man first from the earth, Genesis 2:7 and formed the woman from the side of the man, Genesis 2:21-22. 1 Corinthians 11:7 heightens the importance of the created order of man and woman. Men seem to have some privilege for being made first. The man directly reflects God and the woman reflects the man due to creation sequence.

---

28. Anthony C. Thiselton writes in *1 Corinthians: A Shorter Exegetical & Pastoral Commentary.* Regarding head coverings, "It is beyond doubt that in Roman society a hood (or perhaps a veil) was what a married woman was expected to wear in public as a mark of respectability," page 171.

The word glory - δόξα - *doxa* means dignity.[29]

(Vs. 8) *"For man did not come from woman, but woman from man;"* Paul repeats the creation sequence to build his argument for women covering their heads in order to behave honorably. Maintenance of this creation principle of order in worship assemblies is important to Paul. Order and propriety are intertwined concepts resulting in honor and glory or shame, disgrace and dishonor. Propriety for men and women are important in worship since we are communing with God and fellowshipping with holy people.

(Vs. 9) *"Neither was man created for woman, but woman for man."* God created males and females at different times and for different purposes. Man was created to care for creation (Genesis 2:15) and woman was created to partner with man (Genesis 2:14). Just as the Godhead has different purposes so males and females have different purposes. Different roles or purposes do not determine identity or personhood. Men and women are equal with equal power and spirit. This is demonstrated by the woman coming from the man's side and it is not contradicted by the things Paul says in 1 Corinthians 11.

(Vs. 10) *"It is for this reason that a woman ought to have authority over her own head, because of the angels."* The heavenly host affects the role of women in worship. Much speculation and imagination has occurred in deciphering this verse.[30] What does a woman's head covering have to do with angels? Many have searched for the scriptural relationship between females and angels. We must take into account other texts that speak to this concern as well. But all the arguments are conjecture with thin biblical connections. Tracking Paul's argument that women should cover their heads in worship in this verse seems to be determinative as a significant summation. Paul qualifies his case after this verse with a

29. Bauer, Walter, Arndt, W. F., and Gingrich, F. W., *A Greek-English Lexicon of the New Testament,* revised by F. W. Danker, 3rd ed. (Chicago: University of Chicago Press, 2000).
30. Bruce W. Winter offers an interpretation of "because of the angels" as the gynaikonomos translating "angels" as messengers who spied on the Christians during house church to enforce Roman dress-code laws in *Roman Wives, Roman Widows: The Appearance of the New Women and the Pauline Communities* in chapter 5, page 89. Anthony C. Thiselton writes on page 176 in *1 Corinthians: A Shorter Exegetical & Pastoral Commentary* that "angels" are the heavenly host who model reverence in worship by covering themselves with their wings citing Isaiah 6:2.

statement on mutuality in verses 11 and 12. Winter argues that the entire debate is contextual to the first century regarding Roman laws regulating a woman's wardrobe and the angels are the messengers or gynaikonomos that reported dress code violations to the city magistrates.[31] The angels were not mentioned in the previous list of the spiritual hierarchy in verse 3. Inserting the angels into the discussion seems appropriate since the divine servants are included in the heavenly host. Angels would be placed above humans in the order of creation. (Hebrews 2:7, Psalm 8:5) Arguing that women need to show honor and respect to divine beings during worship seems appropriate. The head covering of women in worship highlights the gender difference between men and women. Who can be sure that a covering communicates anything more than femininity? Many argue the covering should represent subordination but does it? The arguments Paul makes are from the creation narrative in Genesis 1 and 2 but not after the fall and curse of humans in Genesis 3. This is significant since the fall can be read as imposing subordination on women due to the curse, Genesis 3:16 *"To the woman he said, 'I will make your pains in childbearing very severe; with painful labor you will give birth to children. Your desire will be for your husband, and he will rule over you.'"*

(Vs. 11) *"Nevertheless, in the Lord woman is not independent of man, nor is man independent of woman."* We should not confuse "leadership" with "headship." God created males and females in his image with the divine nature. Males and females were created at different times for different reasons. The creation sequence provides theology for our roles and purpose. The creation narrative also provides the theology for our mutuality, sameness, equality, and identity. Dialectic thinking allows for gender distinctions including roles, purpose and propriety to be in tension with equality, sameness and mutuality between males and females. Paul is emphatic in this passage that there is a distinction between genders due to order of creation.

(Vs. 12) *"For as woman came from man, so also man is born of woman. But everything comes from God."* This verse gives balance to the passage by emphasizing the equality and mutuality of males and females. Males and females have an essential sameness of being and spirit. Both were created in the image of God. Men are dependent on women and women

---

31. Bruce W. Winter, pg. 89.

are dependent on men. Males are the seed for life and women are the producers of human life. Both males and females contain the life-giving Spirit of our eternal God. God designed the interdependence of men and women. God wants relationships between men and women to be unified. Men and women should participate in worship with cultural sensitivity so the creation value of "headship" is reflected and symbolized in the way in which each gender conducts themselves. This verse also balances the extreme position of women being subordinate to men. Men and women have different roles as did the Trinity of the Father, Son, and Holy Spirit.

(Vs. 13) *"Judge for yourselves: Is it proper for a woman to pray to God with her head uncovered?"* Paul returns to the primary concern of this pericope, the covering of women's heads in worship. Paul is challenging the Corinthians to answer the question of head coverings for women in worship. Women are to worship in ways that do not dishonor or shame their "head" in the assembly. Paul focuses his audience on the primary issue addressed in this section of the letter. Paul appeals to propriety towards the "head." In this verse the head or object of worship is God. With an understanding of propriety towards God being the issue for men and women in worship it becomes understandable why the apostle is making such a big deal of a covering. Profanity is making the sacred common so Paul is raising the behaviors of men and especially women in Corinth back to a standard of holiness, reverence, spirituality, and sacredness by insisting on propriety.

(Vs. 14) *"Does not the very nature of things teach you that if a man has long hair, it is a disgrace to him."* Paul refers to nature or gender distinction as assumed or obvious to anyone looking around at males and females. The apostle is suggesting that creation indicates a man should not have long hair. Gender distinction should not be blurred and hair length is a marker of gender according to Paul. Long-haired men shame their heads while long-haired women honor their heads. Short-haired women shame their heads and short-haired men honor their heads. Debate over the difference between males and female hair length in the birth and creation process rages. Paul writes as though it is obvious in nature. The length of hair issue could be understood as "cultural" in this context. By "nature" he may have meant by environment or setting.

(Vs. 15) *"But that if a woman has long hair, it is her glory? For long hair is given to her as a covering."* Long hair sets women apart in the created order with beauty and dignity. But long hair is also a covering according to Paul. This concept flies in face of first-century culture as any married woman that let their hair down in Greco/Roman culture for anyone other than her husband was disgraced.[32] Paul may be inferring that since women cannot let their hair down in public as a covering then she should have something to cover her head as was the common practice of the day. But since many contexts allow women to let their hair down in public then long hair can be a covering for women in a context other than 1st century Corinth.

(Vs. 16) *"If anyone wants to be contentious about this, we have no other practice—nor do the churches of God."* Paul returns where he began in this section of the letter by referring to the traditions practiced in the churches. The churches Paul planted were practicing similar customs and patterns of worship. Paul calls the Corinthians to maintain unity within the brotherhood by adhering to common observances. Paul emphasizes his argument by appealing to the practice/tradition of all the Christian churches of the growing movement. Paul's introduction and conclusion in this section exalt the importance of unity within the local church and among the brotherhood of believers. Paul addresses issue after issue in the Corinthian correspondence that was creating division. This pericope is a call to worship with decorum in alignment with heavenly order, created sequence, and sacred propriety.

Reflections

1. Understanding the culture and context of the Corinthian church aids in understanding this passage. Appreciating the themes of 1 Corinthians including unity, cruxiformity, love, and spirituality guides the reading of this pericope. Paul is solving problems and issuing correctives throughout the epistle to form more Christlike disciples in this important city. Paul appreciates the culture and context of the community by advising practices that are coherent with the gospel of Jesus Christ. The apostle issues arguments

---

32. Anthony C. Thiselton writes on page 172 in *1 Corinthians: A Shorter Exegetical & Pastoral Commentary* that having the head uncovered might mean "long, unbound hair, or letting down of the hair" but unlikely.

based on theology from creation to persuade the disciples to unite in worship practices congruent with other Christian communities.

2. This passage is clear regarding the fact that women prayed and prophesied in corporate worship in the first-century church. The pericope is also clear that women should cover their head while praying and prophesying in Corinth and the other churches Paul planted. The application of this passage to another context must not violate the scriptural principles stated in this passage including: (1) Men do not cover your heads in worship; (2) Women cover your heads while praying and prophesying in worship according to the propriety of the context for the sake of unity; (3) Long hair for women is considered a head covering; (4) Women-head covering while praying and prophesying in worship is not merely contextual but rather due to theological arguments from creation. The reasons for head coverings for women from Genesis include creation order, reverence for headship, and created purpose.

3. 1 Corinthians 11:1-16 teaches interdependence and mutuality between men and women while upholding gender distinction between males and females. 1 Corinthians 11:1-16 informs Christians of all cultures and contexts to incorporate women into corporate worship by praying and prophesying or doing something similar in our context. The women participating in corporate worship are to adhere to the theological principles of order, gender propriety, headship, and spiritual reverence. No one, male or female should behave shamefully in worship. Worship is a sacred practice with observance of the headship of God.

4. Decorum in worship is practiced to honor the sacredness of the activity. Reverence demands a posture of humility towards God and mutual respect for one another. Disunity is unacceptable in worship and therefore orderliness is set by creation sequence. Creation order determines roles but not identity. Order is necessary to avoid competition and disunity. Roles are also necessary to avoid competition and disunity.

Bibliography

Bauer, Walter, Arndt, W.F., and Gingrich, F.W., *A Greek-English Lexicon of the New Testament* , revised by F.W. Danker, 3rd ed. (BDAG), (Chicago: University of Chicago Press, 2000).

Bradbury, Rosalene. *Cross Theology: The Classical Theologia Crucis and Karl Barth's Modern Theology of the Cross,* James Clarke & Co Ltd. (2012).

Fee, Gordon D. *The First Epistle to the Corinthians.* Grand Rapids: Eerdmans, 1987.

Fee, Gordon D. "Praying and Propheseying in the Assemblies: 1 Corinthians 11:2-16" pg. 142-160. In Pierce, R. W., Groothuis, R. M., & Fee, G. D. (2005). *Discovering biblical equality: Complementarity without hierarchy.* Downers Grove, IL: InterVarsity Press.

Liddell, Henry George. and Scott, Robert. *A Greek-English Lexicon.* Oxford: Clarendon, 1996.

Lee-Barnewall, Michelle. *Neither Complementarian nor Egalitarian: A Kingdom Corrective to the Evangelical Gender Debate.* Grand Rapids, MI: Baker Academic, 2016.

Louw, Johannes P. and Nida, Eugene A. (editors of *Greek-English Lexicon of the New Testament Based on Semantic Domains,* second edition. New York, United Bible Societies, 1989.

Nichols, David R. "The Problem of Two-Level Christianity at Corinth." *Pneuma: The Journal of the Society for Pentecostal Studies* 11, no. 2 (fall 1989): 99-111.

Pierce, R. W., Groothuis, R. M., & Fee, G. D. (2005). *Discovering biblical equality: Complementarity without hierarchy.* Downers Grove, IL: InterVarsity Press.

Robinson, Edward. *A Greek and English Lexicon of the New Testament* (Boston and New York: Houghton, Mifflin and Company, 1887

Schreiner, Thomas R. in chapter 5 "Head Coverings, Prophecies, and the Trinity: 1 Corinthians 11:2-16" In John Piper & Wayne Grudem, *Recovering Biblical Manhood & Womanhood* (p. 124-139). Wheaton, IL: Crossway Books.

Thayer, J. H. *The New Greek-English Lexicon of the New Testament,* Peabody, MA: Hendrickson, 1981.

Thiselton, Anthony C. *1 Corinthians: A Shorter Exegetical & Pastoral Commentary.* Eerdmans: Grand Rapids, MI, 2006.

Williams, H. H. D. "Living as Christ Crucified: The Cross as a Foundation for Christian Ethics in 1 Corinthians." *Evangelical Quarterly* 75, no. 2 (2003): 117-31.

Witherington, Ben, III. *Conflict and Community in Corinth: A Socio-Rhetorical Commentary on 1 and 2 Corinthians.* Grand Rapids: Eerdmans, 1995.

Winter, Bruce W. Roman Wives, *Roman Widows: The Appearance of the New Women and the Pauline Communities.* Grand Rapids: Eerdmans, 2003.

CHAPTER THREE

1 Corinthians 14:33-40

By Dr. Gregg Marutzky

1 Corinthians 14:33-40 *"[33]For God is not a God of disorder but of peace—as in all the congregations of the Lord's people. [34]Women should remain silent in the churches. They are not allowed to speak, but must be in submission, as the law says. [35]If they want to inquire about something, they should ask their own husbands at home; for it is disgraceful for a woman to speak in the church. [36]Or did the word of God originate with you? Or are you the only people it has reached? [37]If anyone thinks they are a prophet or otherwise gifted by the Spirit, let them acknowledge that what I am writing to you is the Lord's command. [38]But if anyone ignores this, they will themselves be ignored. [39]Therefore, my brothers and sisters, be eager to prophesy, and do not forbid speaking in tongues. [40]But everything should be done in a fitting and orderly way." (NIV, 2011)*[33]

Introduction

The passage of 1 Corinthians 14:33-40 is important for an understanding of women's role in the church. The declaration that "women are to be silent in the church" must be reconciled with instructions for women to sing, pray, and prophesy in the corporate worship. The culture of the first century informs the understanding of this passage. Also, the context of the pericope guides the interpretation of debatable issues. Are women to never speak in the church? Is the instruction to remain silent during the entire worship service? Does submission mean to not speak and remain silent? What if a woman does not have a husband to ask questions at home after the worship service? Many questions are raised from this passage.

---

33. All references unless otherwise noted are from NIV, 2011.

Corinthian Correspondence

1. The building up of the body of Christ is a theme in the Corinthian correspondence. Paul addresses issues contributing to disunity among the Corinthian disciples. (1 Corinthians 1:11).

2. Paul instructs the Corinthians regarding true spirituality as cruciform living (1 Corinthians 1-3) and practicing the ethic of love towards everyone especially Christian brothers and sisters (1 Corinthians 13).

3. The Corinthians correspondence seeks to bring unity to a divided church and redefine spirituality through the theology of the Cross and the gospel of Jesus Christ (1 Corinthians 1:18).[34] The language of the letter shifts between instruction to correction, affirmation to admonishment.

4. Several issues are producing disunity in the Corinthian church including immorality (chapter 5), lawsuits (chapter 6), divorce (chapter 7), non-Kosher food (chapter 8), Lord's Supper (chapter 11), spiritual gifts (chapter 12), resurrection (chapter 15), and money (chapter 16).

5. Conduct in corporate worship is a primary concern for the Apostle Paul including sharing of the Lord's Supper, women's role, proper expression of spiritual gifts, mutual respect, unity, decorum, and glorification of God (1 Corinthians 11-14).

6. Corporate assemblies follow theological teaching and guiding principles. Theological principles include the heavenly hierarchy, order of creation, gender roles, and purity codes. Guiding principles include propriety, order, peace, unity, and mutual respect. Paul expresses definitive language in Corinthians when he wants to correct the church (1 Corinthians 11-14).

Culture

The key to understanding 1 Corinthians 14:33-40 is an understanding of the first-century culture regarding gender and social expectations for honorable women. Corinth was a Greco-Roman city that was heavily influenced by the mores of Hellenization that regulated

---

34. Williams, H. H. D. "Living as Christ Crucified: The Cross as a Foundation for Christian Ethics in 1 Corinthians." *Evangelical Quarterly* 75, no. 2 (2003): 117-31.

the status of women as subservient to men due to the philosophical writings of Plato and Aristotle.[35] The culture was an honor/shame society that defined honor and virtue according to ancient Greek philosophy. A virtuous woman practiced a code of honor. An honorable woman in Greco-Roman society followed prescriptions that were being challenged by the "New Roman Woman" that tested the social codes for female behavior.[36]

The expectations for an honorable woman were to dress appropriately in public and to be accompanied by their husband. Most importantly for the understanding of this passage was the social code for women to be silent in mixed company with men and women. Women were expected to remain silent among men who were not their husbands while in public.[37] Honorable women conversed with their husbands in the private setting of their homes. The dichotomy between public and private was significant regarding the acceptability of behavior for women. Women were expected to maintain privacy regarding their dress, speech, and activity. Women were confined to private spaces and were limited in the public sphere in the ancient world. Roman society upheld many of the Grecian social codes but there is some historical evidence that a feminist movement to elevate the status of women was also occurring in the first century.[38]

Context

The context of the verses under discussion is found among instructions regarding public worship with a focus on the speaking of tongues and prophesying (vs. 4). Tongue speakers are overlapping with one another (vs. 27). Multiple speakers are expressing their gift of

35. Cawthon, D. (2017). The philosophical foundations of leadership. New York, NY: Routledge Taylor & Francis Group.
36. Winter, Bruce W. (2003). *"Roman Wives, Roman Widows: The Appearance of the New Women and the Pauline Communities."* Winter describes the first-century culture regarding women and proposes a feminist movement described as the "New Roman Woman."
37. Valerius Maximus, Memorable Doings and Sayings, III.8.6, "What business has a woman with a public meeting? If ancestral custom is observed, none."
38. deSilva, D. A. (2000). *"Honor, patronage, kinship & purity: Unlocking New Testament culture."* deSilva provides a comprehensive description of the honor/shame culture of the first century and the purity codes of the Greco/Roman culture.

prophecy or the gift of speaking in tongues at the same time producing confusion (vs. 29). The interpretation of the tongues does not always occur (vs. 13). The service seems to degenerate into chaos with the different gifts being expressed simultaneously. Therefore the Apostle Paul instructs the Corinthians to impose some organization and structure into their services (vss. 31-32). He provides guiding principles for the practice of corporate worship. Guiding principles include to build up and edify the church (vs. 12, 26), plus worship with order and propriety (vs. 33). Paul provides guidance that tongue-speaking should be accompanied by interpretation (vs. 28). The distinction between the spirit and the mind is useful in understanding edification and meaning (vs. 14-15). The mind must be engaged for both edification and meaning to occur.

The guiding principle of building up the body prohibits practices that exclude others in corporate worship especially visitors and guests (vss. 24-25). Worship should reveal God to all people and not exclude seekers or unbelievers. Worship in the assembly includes praising God, edification of the believer, understandability for visitors. Personal edification occurs in tongue-speaking without meaning but not communal edification (vs. 17). Paul boldly pronounces judgment on tongue-speaking in corporate worship if it is not accompanied by interpretation (vss. 18-19). Paul describes tongue speaking as an exclusive practice in corporate worship if interpretation does not occur. Paul accuses the Corinthians of thinking like children (vs. 20). He is boldly challenging the church to grow up spiritually and not compete in exercising their gifts. Tongues are used to witness to unbelievers in reference to speaking the Word of God in the language of the unbeliever while prophecy is for believers (vs. 22). Speaking in a foreign language to people who do not speak that language is fruitless (vs. 10, 21). Without understanding there is no meaning. Ecstatic utterances and emotional rambling results in seekers hearing nothing meaningful (vs. 23). Preaching God's word and prophecy convicts listeners of sin through the power of the Holy Spirit (vs. 24). Worship is the natural response to revelation (vs. 25). When God is revealed we prostrate ourselves in reverence and praise. The word of God judges the secrets of our hearts and produces conviction plus awe of God. The presence of God is recognized through conviction rather than by ecstasy.

"Everything must be done so that the church may be built up" (vs.

26) is a guiding principle to build up the church.[39] Paul is bold when he addresses issues that tear down the church and calls for singing, teaching, revelation, preaching, and tongues with interpretation only be practiced in the church for edification. Paul provides practical guidance for the speaking in tongues in corporate worship with only three people allowed to speak in the assembly in one service. Silence and personal edification must be practiced in the church by tongue-speakers if there is no interpretation. Paul also allowed only three prophets to speak in the corporate worship. The church should "weigh" or analyze/examine the prophecy to determine the validity of the message. Protocol and decorum are required in the church with never two speakers at the same time. Respect for the speaker is foremost in worship. Paul confirms that the prophet must exercise self-control in sharing prophecy. The Spirit does not take over a person or deny his or her free will.

Exegesis of 1 Corinthians 14:33-38, Women Keeping Silent in the Church:

1 Corinthians 14:33 *"For God is not a God of disorder but of peace—as in all the congregations of the Lord's people."* Paul provides another guiding principle for corporate worship. The requirement is a decorum of peace and order. Disunity, disorder, and chaos are antithetical in Christian worship. The context of Paul's instruction in this chapter is public worship as he states in verse 33b, "as in all the congregations of the Lord's people." Scholars debate the placement of this verse. Most manuscripts have the placement as verse 33b but some manuscripts place the phrase after verse 34. But regardless of its original location in the manuscript, peace and order are the decorum of worship.

There is also debate about whether Paul wrote these few verses due to late manuscript evidence but the text seems accurate as it currently stands. Paul is convinced that the goal of edification necessitates some "order" (14:40) in the assembly activities because God is a God of order and peace rather than disorder (14:33). Paul corrects the kinds of disorder in this text. Silence is appropriate in specific situations to maintain propriety and order, which is alluded to in verse 35. Men and women should not act in a disorderly or disruptive manner.

---

39. Lee-Barnewall, M. (2016). *"Neither Complementarian nor Egalitarian: A Kingdom Corrective to the Evangelical Gender Debate."* p. 90.

1 Corinthians 14:34 *"Women should remain silent in the churches. They are not allowed to speak, but must be in submission, as the law says."* The prohibition for women speaking in tongues or prophesying in the church is declarative. "Women should remain silent." (Greek silent *"sigatosin"*) The Greek verb, σιγάω, *sigao,* "to be silent" is used three times in 1 Corinthians 14 including verse 28, "if there is no one to interpret, let each of them keep silent," also in verse 30, "if a revelation is made ... let the first be silent," finally in verse 34, "women should remain silent."[40] In verse 34 the verb is a present infinitive tense meaning to stop continual talk or disruptive speech. The call for silence can refer to literal silence or to be quiet and wait your turn. The instruction follows the theme of the entire chapter to maintain order. Considering the context of the three uses of the word silence in this chapter the declaration is not for the women to always be silent in the church but rather at a certain time and situation. The other references in the passage call for temporary silence not ongoing, absolute silence.

Paul corrects three kinds of disorder in this text. First, tongue speakers were speaking without interpreters and they were all speaking at once. Paul wants only two (and at the most three) to speak. If there is no interpreter, then the tongue speaker should be silent (14:28). Tongue speakers should control themselves. Second, prophets should control themselves and speak in some kind of order. Two or three should speak while the other prophets judge their prophecies. If any prophet receives a revelation, the others should be silent (14:30). Third, women should respect order and not disrupt the assembly. There is a time for silence in the service. Speakers should remain silent while others are speaking and women are to remain silent if not directed to pray and prophesy. Women are to remain silent in the critique of the prophets. Women do not have to be completely silent but they do sing, pray, and speak just as the tongue speakers and prophets could sing, pray, and speak when it was their turn. Silence is expected in specific situations, which is referenced in verse 35. Women should not act in an improper or disruptive manner.[41]

---

40. BDAG, Bauer, Walter, Arndt, W. F., and Gingrich, F. W. (2000). *A Greek-English Lexicon of the New Testament.*

41. Witherington, B. III. (1995), *"Conflict and Community in Corinth: A Socio-Rhetorical Commentary on 1 and 2 Corinthians."* p. 287.

The debate among scholars is the call for the silence of women. The debate centers on what speech the women must cease. In context the issue seems to be disorderly or disruptive speech (vs. 40). But if total silence were the declaration then the instruction in 1 Corinthians 11:4 where women are instructed how to pray and prophesy would be unnecessary. Women absolutely sang, prayed, and prophesied in the early church so a moratorium on silence is indefensible. But women clearly were to be silent according to verse 34 for particular reasons and specific situations in the Corinthian church.

In each case Paul is correcting disruptive activity. Stop speaking over one another, stop interrupting each other, and wait your turn. So it seems to follow that Paul is instructing the women to not be disruptive. Paul has already explained the necessity for women to be under the authority of God in worship and to practice a supportive role while maintaining order. (See 1 Corinthians 11:1-16) Paul is applying the principle of order to the speech of the women in the corporate worship in these verses. The disorder of the Corinthians must be corrected so the apostle's language is direct and declarative. God is a God of order in all the assemblies of the church. Part of the "order" is that women act consistently with the "law." The interpretive options of the law include the Old Testament, Roman law, or Greco-Roman tradition (Carson, 1991). The law or proper action infers women act in a submissive manner according to appropriate behavior for a honorable or virtuous woman. Order means that women do not violate God's intention for "divine headship" which Paul has already discussed in 11:3-10. The Corinthian women were violating that "order" and thus Paul wants them to stop speaking in disruptive or insubmissive ways.

1 Corinthians 14:35 *"If they want to inquire about something, they should ask their own husbands at home; for it is disgraceful for a woman to speak in the church."* This verse refers to the cultural practice for women to remain predominantly in private and to restrict their interaction with men in public. Paul condemns disgraceful speech by women in the fellowship. Interestingly he does not say sinful speech but rather inappropriate speech. It definitely was inappropriate in the first century for a woman to correct a man in public.[42] Therefore if the women were trying to critique

---

42. The Digest 16.1.2 (Ulpian), It was against Roman law for a woman to publicly intervene for her husband in a legal argument.

the male tongue-speakers or prophets then that behavior would be considered disgraceful.[43] In public the custom in Greco-Roman society was for honorable women to seldom venture out from the private sphere. The virtuous Greek woman maintain a propriety of dress and speech in public that followed cultural norms that were established codes of conduct.[44]

Some scholars propose this verse refers to Genesis 3:16, "To the woman he said, 'I will make your pains in childbearing very severe; with painful labor you will give birth to children. Your desire will be for your husband, and he will rule over you" which is often used to reinforce the household hierarchy of women being submissive to men. Another interpretation describes that women and men will no longer be harmonious but rather contend with one another. The curse describes the result of the fall but not God's desired will for humankind. Unfortunately the fall produced a struggle between men and women with the genders seeking to dominate each other. An interpretation of the Hebrew that describes the struggle reads, "you will want to dominate your husband and he will seek to rule over you."[45] Christ came to redeem us from the fall. Christ initiated the new age that will reverse the fall with the full realization of the new age with a new heaven and a new earth.[46]

1 Corinthians 14:36 *"Or did the word of God originate with you? Or are you the only people it has reached?"* Paul reminds the Corinthians of their place in the big picture. It seems they were thinking too highly of themselves. Spiritual pride is divisive and arrogant. The Corinthians are not the standard (14:36—the word of God did not originate with them, nor are they the only recipients of the word). It seems Paul commands women to be totally silent in the assembly (e.g., no singing, no confessing, no praying, etc.), but this does not recognize the specific situation of this text and it contradicts 11:3-6. The verse prohibits women from either

43. Fee, Gordon D. *"Equality with or without innocence: Genesis 1-3"* pg. 79-93. In Pierce, R. W., Groothuis, R. M., & Fee, G. D. Discovering biblical equality: Complementarity without hierarchy. Downers Grove, IL: InterVarsity Press 2005.

44. deSilva, 2000, p. 231.

45. Hess, R. *"Praying and Prophesying in the Assemblies: 1 Corinthians 11:2-16."* (2005), p. 92.

46. N.T. Wright describe the realized eschatology Christ initiated in his book, "Surprised by Hope" (2008). The second coming of Christ will heal the world of the fall and the curses will no longer effect males, females, and creation.

or all of the following: (1) asking their husbands questions during their prophesying, or (2) disrupting the judging of the prophets by asking questions, or (3) disrupting the assembly by insubmissive behavior. Paul's interpretation of the law does not command silence; rather, it seems to imply submission. Silence is an application of the principle of submission in this specific situation due to disorderly conduct.[47]

1 Corinthians 14:37 *"If anyone thinks they are a prophet or otherwise gifted by the Spirit, let them acknowledge that what I am writing to you is the Lord's command."* True prophets were to confirm Paul's instructions as inspired by God or Paul considers them false prophets. Paul recognizes he is correcting the Corinthians so he invokes the authority of God's commandment. Disorder, confusion, and disunity are not acceptable during worship. Reverence, respect, peace, and humility are expected in God's presence. Disgraceful, disruptive, disorderly, disunifying activity is intolerable for corporate assemblies. Differing views on the role of women in worship must not violate the priority of unity among disciples of Christ and especially in the corporate assembly.

1 Corinthians 14:38 *"But if anyone ignores this, they will themselves be ignored."* Paul exercises his authority as an apostle by issuing judgment upon anyone who would reject this instruction. Paul persuades, pleads and preaches throughout the Corinthian correspondence, varying his statements according to the whether the material is corrective, instructive, or affirmative. In this case Paul is corrective and declarative with direct language to align the practices of the Corinthian church with the other first-century fellowships. Paul seems passionate to correct the disorder and disarray of the Corinthian worship assembly.

1 Corinthians 14:39 *"Therefore, my brothers and sisters, be eager to prophesy, and do not forbid speaking in tongues."* This verse returns to the original subject of the chapter summarizing Paul's direction to emphasize prophecy in worship for the sake of mutual edification and minimize tongue speaking especially without interpretation. Tongues speaking and prophecy are beyond the scope of this paper.

1 Corinthians 14:40 *"But everything should be done in a fitting and orderly way."* Finally Paul reiterates the guiding principle for worship to be

---

47. Thiselton, A. (2006). *"1 Corinthians: A Shorter Exegetical & Pastoral Commentary.*

conducted appropriately, orderly, and in a disciplined manner. Verses 33-40 seem to be a unit since worship order begins and ends the section.

Reflections

1. Immediately following the definition of love in 1 Corinthians 13, Paul applies the virtue of love to instructions regarding corporate worship in 1 Corinthians 14.

2. The issue in 1 Corinthians 14 is the misuse of spiritual gifts and the lack of mutual respect for one another.

3. Paul declares the guiding principles of peace and order be practiced in corporate assemblies.

4. Women are directed to maintain a supporting role in worship and not usurp the leadership.

5. Women do not remain absolutely silent in worship but participate fully, limited only by a call to practice propriety in worship.

6. Brotherhood unity is addressed by Paul's correction of the Corinthian church highlighting the necessity of individual churches not observing disruptive worship practices.

7. The concept of order is paramount in Paul's teaching regarding corporate worship to alleviate disunity, power struggles, and conflict especially regarding gender-specific roles.

Bibliography

BDAG, Bauer, Walter, Arndt, W.F., and Gingrich, F.W., *A Greek-English Lexicon of the New Testament,* revised by F.W. Danker, 3rd ed. (Chicago: University of Chicago Press, 2000).

Carson, D. A. in chapter 6 "Silent in the Churches: On the role of women in 1 Corinthians 14:33b-36" In John Piper & Wayne Grudem, ed. *Recovering Biblical Manhood & Womanhood* (p. 140-153). Wheaton, IL: Crossway Books, 1991.

Cawthon, D. (2017). *The philosophical foundations of leadership.* New York, NY: Routledge Taylor & Francis Group.

deSilva, D. A. (2000). *Honor, patronage, kinship & purity: Unlocking New Testament culture.* Downers Grove, IL: InterVarsity Press.

Fee, Gordon D."Equality with or without innocence: Genesis 1-3" pg. 79-93. In Pierce, R. W., Groothuis, R. M., & Fee, G. D. *Discovering biblical equality: Complementarity without hierarchy.* Downers Grove, IL: InterVarsity Press 2005.

Hess, Richard S. *"Praying and Propheseying in the Assemblies: 1 Corinthians 11:2-16"* pg. 161-171. In Pierce, R. W., Groothuis, R. M., & Fee, G. D. *Discovering biblical equality: Complementarity without hierarchy.* Downers Grove, IL: InterVarsity Press, 2005.

Lee-Barnewall, Michelle. *Neither Complementarian nor Egalitarian: A Kingdom Corrective to the Evangelical Gender Debate.* Grand Rapids, MI: Baker Academic, 2016.

Thiselton, Anthony C. *1 Corinthians: A Shorter Exegetical & Pastoral Commentary.* Eerdmans: Grand Rapids, MI, 2006.

Williams, H. H. D. "Living as Christ Crucified: The Cross as a Foundation for Christian Ethics in 1 Corinthians." *Evangelical Quarterly* 75, no. 2 (2003): 117-31.

Witherington, Ben, III. *Conflict and Community in Corinth: A Socio-Rhetorical Commentary on 1 and 2 Corinthians.* Grand Rapids: Eerdmans, 1995.

Winter, Bruce W. *Roman Wives, Roman Widows: The Appearance of the New Women and the Pauline Communities.* Grand Rapids: Eerdmans, 2003.

Wright, N. T., *"Surprised by Hope: Rethinking Heaven, the Resurrection, and the Mission of the Church."* HarperCollins Publishing, New York. (2008).

All One in Christ Jesus
Galatians 3:26–29

Valdur Koha

Abstract

Galatians 3:26–29 is one of the passages often cited in the context of gender discussions in the church. In this paper an attempt is made to describe how the passage ought to be interpreted in the context of the overall letter, the immediate context of the section (i.e., vv. 3:19–25 and 4:1–11), and Paul's theology.

Galatians 3:26–29

26So in Christ Jesus you are all children of God through faith, 27for all of you who were baptized into Christ have clothed yourselves with Christ. 28There is neither Jew nor Gentile, neither slave nor free, nor is there male and female, for you are all one in Christ Jesus. 29If you belong to Christ, then you are Abraham's seed, and heirs according to the promise. (NIV2011)

This passage represents certainly one of the most inspiring texts in all of Paul's writing. There might be no more compact and exciting summary of God's plan of salvation and vision for God's people than these four verses!

Verse 28 in particular has gained much prominence in the contemporary debate over the roles of men and women in the church, in the home, and in the society. For example, the web page of Christians for Biblical Equality states, "Christians for Biblical Equality is an organization of Christians who believe the Bible, properly interpreted, teaches the fundamental equality of men and women of all racial and ethnic groups, all economic classes, and all age groups, based on biblical teachings summarized in Galatians 3:28" (www.cbeinternational.org).

Rebecca Groothuis writes, "Of all the texts that support biblical equality, Galatians 3:26–28 is probably the most important" (Groothuis, 1997). For some, Galatians 3:28 is more than a key text in the debate over men's and women's roles in the home and church; rather, it is the fundamental or most important statement in the New Testament on this issue (Hove, 1999).

There are, of course, those who disagree with this assessment. They believe Galatians 3:28 says little about gender-based roles in the church: "Paul's statement is not concerned with the role relationships of men and women within the Body of Christ but rather with their common initiation/integration into it through faith and baptism" (Fung, 1987).

Considering the context, our approach is "outside in," beginning with the overall letter, exploring the immediate context, and seeking to understand how the four verses, 26–29, fit within the letter.

Paul's Letter to the Galatians

The apostle Paul wrote the letter to the churches in southern Galatia, and perhaps northern Galatia, which he had founded on his missionary journeys. It is an intense letter, as Paul is very concerned to counter the claims of some Judeans (probably Jewish Christians) who were telling the Galatian Gentile Christians that they must be circumcised and keep the Law of Moses in order to truly belong to God's people. Most likely the letter was written rather early, around AD 48.

In the introduction of the letter, Paul defends his office and authority as apostle of Christ Jesus (1:1) and makes it clear that he has received the gospel as revelation from Jesus Christ (1:11). Paul's emphasis of the source of his convictions as well as the strong characterization of the teaching as "perverted gospel" (1:7) demonstrate the importance that he accords his letter. His emotional outbursts—"I am astonished ..." (v. 1:6), "You foolish Galatians!" (v. 3:1), "I fear for you ..." (4:11), "I plead with you ..." (v. 4:12), "I am perplexed about you!" (v. 4:20), "See what large letters I use ..." (v. 6:11)—demonstrate the intensity of the letter. Paul's concern is not the correction of flawed church practices or a thesis of overall church doctrine. He has a laser-sharp focus on false teachings that infiltrated the Galatian churches, completely perverting the true meaning of the gospel, to the point that it makes it "no gospel at all" (1:7).

On the highest level, the issue that Paul deals with throughout the letter is the relationship between what God has done in Christ and what God had already done in and with Israel (Longenecker, 1998, 17).

The six short chapters contain a very focused message. Paul addresses one major and overriding concern. In his arrangement of arguments, he develops a number of important theological concepts, but he is uniquely focused on addressing the false teaching that has been brought into the churches. Paul was shocked and greatly disturbed at what he had learned about his converts in Galatia since leaving them (1:6). We have no description of the false teaching and have to draw our conclusions from Paul's passionate response to what he heard from the Galatian churches (it seems that he had no direct exchange with the false teachers himself). This attempt at mirror-reading is imprecise and is one area of disagreement in the interpretations of the letter. Making too much out of speculation about the situation in Galatia, going outside of what the text says, is misleading at best.

The message of the false teachers includes as key points: (1) Circumcision is the manner by which one joins the family of Abraham and becomes an heir of the promise given to Abraham. (2) Christ's death allows both Jews and Gentiles to enter together anew into the historic covenant God has made with his people, the Torah, which is God's gift to all who would "choose life." (3) The Torah is God's gracious provision for us to make progress in our life in Christ and in our struggle to master the passions of the flesh and to experience freedom from their power over us (DeSilva, 2018).

At the core of the struggle is Paul's conviction of the existence of two worlds: the obliteration of one "world" and its replacement by another. This transformation of the individual, the community, and ultimately the world is one of the key tenets of Paul's theological understanding. On one side is the old world, fallen and dominated by enemies of God and the powers of death, sin, and the flesh. The new world is the redeemed created order, which God has inaugurated in Christ. The ages of the old and the new overlap—the new is here "already" and "not yet." In Galatians, Paul evidences little interest in the future manifestation of God's triumph. Instead, the focus is on the eschatological present (Longenecker, 1990, 6).

We'll analyze the structure of the letter and the immediate context before interpreting Galatians 3:26–29.

Structure of the Letter

A good overview of the letter can be given through the description of five structural segments (based on Krimmer, 2018).

I. Introduction (1:1–10)
A. Paul and his recipients (1:1–2)
B. Praise for God (1:3–5)
C. Against the distortion of the gospel (1:6–10)

II. Threefold authorization of Paul as apostle by God himself (1:11–2:21)
A. Called by Christ himself (1:11–17)
B. Acknowledged and respected by the other apostles and brothers (1:18–2:10)
C. Paul's commission and Peter (2:11–21)

III. The core of Paul's argument or "the dogmatical part" (3:1–5:12)
A. The blindness of the Galatians (3:1–5).
B. The blessing of the faith versus the curse of the Law (3:6–14)
C. The purpose of the Law (3:15–25)
D. ➡ **The coming of the faith (3:26–29)**
E. Heirs coming of age (4:1–7)
F. Pastoral encouragement in love (4:8–20)
G. A biblical allegory for the relationship between law and promise (4:21–31)
H. An appeal to true freedom (5:1–12)

IV. The proper use of freedom in Christ (5:13–6:10)
A. Freedom empowers service in love (5:13–15)
B. Life in the Spirit (5:16–25)
C. Fellowship with one another (5:26–6:5)
D. Mutual support (6:6–10)

V. Paul's parting thoughts and affirmations (6:11–18)

The text of our investigation we call here "the coming of [the] faith" (3:23). Arguably, 3:26–29 represents the pivotal, climactic center of the letter (Das, 2014, 377). The text is almost exactly in the midpoint of the letter when counting verses: Galatians 3:29 is the 74th verse of the letter followed by 75 verses to the end.

Immediate Context

The immediate context of Galatians 3:26–29 consists of verses 3:19–25 before and 4:1–7 after. The sequence of units of thought is therefore:

1. The Purpose of the Law (3:19–25)

2. The Coming of the Faith (3:26–29)

3. Heirs Coming of Age (4:1–11)

Let's look at 3:19–25 and 4:1–7 before analyzing verses 26–29. The section leading up to our paragraph addresses the question of the purpose of the Law at the time before the coming of the faith:

Galatians 3:19–25

[19]Why, then, was the law given at all? It was added because of transgressions until the Seed to whom the promise referred had come. The law was given through angels and entrusted to a mediator. [20]A mediator, however, implies more than one party; but God is one.

[21]Is the law, therefore, opposed to the promises of God? Absolutely not! For if a law had been given that could impart life, then righteousness would certainly have come by the law. [22]But Scripture has locked up everything under the control of sin, so that what was promised, being given through faith in Jesus Christ, might be given to those who believe.

[23]Before the coming of this faith, we were held in custody under the law, locked up until the faith that was to come would be revealed. [24]So the law was our guardian until Christ came that we might be justified by faith. 25 Now that this faith has come, we are no longer under a guardian. (NIV2011)

Paul describes the temporary nature of the law as well as the limits of its value. He uses the image of a "guardian" to describe the law. A better term is probably "pedagogue" (DeSilva, 2018, 329) or a disciplinarian over younger children whose role changes or disappears when the children grow up.

Longenecker (1990, 146ff.) calls παιδαγωγὸς (*paidagogos*) a "supervisory guardian." He writes, "Paul's use of the term παιδαγωγὸς has often puzzled commentators. For while today we think of pedagogues as teachers, in antiquity a *paidagogos* was distinguished from a *didaskalos* ('teacher') and had custodial and disciplinary functions rather than educative or instructional ones."

Martyn (1997, 363) calls the Law "an imprisoning warden," stating that Paul is using *paidagogos* in the sense of a distinctly unfriendly and confining custodian, different in no significant way from an imprisoning jailer.

The paragraph (3:19–25) ends in verse 25 with "but now that this faith has come, we are no longer under a supervising guardian." Here Paul delivers the coup de grace to the Judaizers' argument for Gentile Christians to live a lifestyle governed by the Mosaic law. For with the coming of the Christian gospel as effected by Christ, the law no longer has validity as παιδαγωγὸς regulating the life of faith (Longenecker 1990, 149). To be a Jewish Christian does not mean having to give up Jewish culture or customs. However, it was completely unacceptable to demand any Jewish legal requirements, customs, or traditions (circumcision, food, or anything else) as a requirement for becoming or being a member of God's people. This is the context immediately preceding the four verses of our study.

The unit of thought after paragraph 3:26–29 consists of 4:1–7.

Galatians 4:1–7

> [1]What I am saying is that as long as an heir is underage, he is no different from a slave, although he owns the whole estate. [2]The heir is subject to guardians and trustees until the time set by his father. [3]So also, when we were underage, we were in slavery under the elemental spiritual forces of the world. [4]But when the set time had fully come, God sent his Son, born of a woman, born under the law, [5]to redeem those under the law, that we might receive adoption to sonship. [6]Because you are his sons, God sent the Spirit of his Son into our hearts, the Spirit who calls out, "Abba, Father." [7]So you are no longer a slave, but God's child; and since you are his child, God has made you also an heir. (NIV2011)

Here is a description of heirs who have come of age. It is a continuation or restatement of the text before verses 26–29. A parallel is drawn between growing up and gaining freedom from slavery. Freedom in Christ brings sonship with God.

The contrast between the underage and the fully entitled child, between slave and son, stands for the contrast between the law and the faith. The question is again: How do I become the fully entitled child of God? Is it really only possible by keeping the law, as the false teachers want to tell the insecure Galatians?

Paul uses here an example from the domain of Hellenistic law, with which the Galatians must have been familiar. He describes a child (whose dad may have passed away) who has not yet come of age. The child is the heir already but legally still a minor. As such he has the state of a slave when it comes to his access over the inherited possessions. However, his father determined the date at which the child will gain the status of a full heir. This is how God treats us. When we were slaves, he determined the time to make us sons; this is the gospel of Jesus Christ. The progression is from slave to son or daughter, and from son or daughter to heir who has come of age. This inspiring illustration repeats and confirms the text of verses 26–29.

Exegesis of Galatians 3:26–29

The coming of the faith replaces the law and brings justification before God. Verses 26 to 29 describe a self-contained thought unit that is at the core of Paul's argument in the letter.

It is important to realize that the popular verse 28 is in context not an isolated saying but rather an integral part of a larger argument that is framed by two clauses in verses 26, 27 and 29, "You are all children… and… you are Abraham's seed" (Hove, 52). Also, verse 26 shifts (in the Greek as in the translation) the pronouns to the second person— the preceding section (3:23–25) is in the first person and the following section (4:1–2) begins in the third person, moves to the first (4:3–5) and ends back in the second (4:6–7). This not only characterizes the thought unit but also directs the inspiring identification to the Galatians.

Galatians 3:26

So in Christ Jesus you are all children of God through faith (NIV2011)

For you are all sons and daughters of God in Christ Jesus through faith. (DeSilva, 2018)

For you are – all of you – sons of God through the faith that is in Christ Jesus. (Martyn, J. L., 1997)

English translations that render 3:26 as "You are all sons and daughters of God through faith in Christ Jesus" (e.g., CEB, NLT) obscure the possibility that Paul intends the two prepositional phrases—"through trust" and "in Christ Jesus"—to be understood separately, making two distinct affirmations in parallel fashion: "You are God's sons and daughters by means of trust" and "You are sons and daughters in Christ Jesus," that is, as believers enter "into" Christ and wrap Christ around them in the rite of baptism (DeSilva, 2018, 336).

The key point of the statement lies in the status of Christians as children of God. The switch to "you" also indicates the need for God's children to accept this status—by faith. God does not force the adoption of his sons and daughters. "Yet to all who did receive him, to those who believed in his name, he gave the right to become children of God—children born not of natural descent, nor of human decision or a husband's will, but born of God" (John 1:12–13, NIV2011).

The universal nature of the statement "You are all children of God" would probably have been startling to the Galatians. Paul declares that all Galatians, Jews and Gentiles alike, are sons of God. "Sons" includes males and females, which leads translators to use "sons and daughters" or "children." This could cause some confusion in chapter 4:4–7, where Paul makes the connection between God's Son and our inheritance/ status as "sons." But it seems clear what Paul means.

"In Christ Jesus" is a well-used Pauline expression and a key concept not only for this passage but for the entire book of Galatians. Sonship is available only in God's Son, in Christ. "It is because he [Christ] has entered our family that we enter the family of God (Hebrews 2:5–18)" (Ferguson, 1986).

"No statement more powerfully sums up Paul's notion of the Christian life than that which forms the climax of one of his greatest arguments in Galatians: 'You are all sons of God through faith in Christ Jesus'" (Kennedy, 1919, 106).

Galatians 3:27

For all of you who were baptized into Christ have clothed yourselves with Christ. (NIV2011)

Verse 27 clarifies verse 26 by using two images to describe "in Christ Jesus": baptism and clothing. Baptism is so closely aligned with salvation in the New Testament that often baptism can, by metonymy, stand for the whole conversion experience (Hove, 1999).

Clothing with Christ is also an image that is used in the New Testament to describe the new life in Christ (Romans 13:14; Ephesians 4:24; Colossians 3:10). Such new clothes stand also for a new identity of the believers and may symbolize an outward description of the unity of all the Christians.

Galatians 3:28

There is neither Jew nor Gentile, neither slave nor free, nor is there male and female, for you are all one in Christ Jesus. (NIV2011)

Verse 28 is the core of our considerations. It consists of three pairs and a final clause, which provides the reason for the negation of the pairs. The syntax of the verse is simple, but the meaning and significance is disputed. Many scholars think this is a baptism formula or a creed, (Betz, 1979 or Longenecker, 1990). There are parallels in Paul's writings (1 Corinthians 12:13; Colossians 3:11), but they don't mention the male/female pair. It seems inappropriate to put much weight on the possibility of a baptismal formula or a creed.

There is neither Jew nor Gentile: The elimination of the social value of the first pair is of obvious relevance to the situation in Galatia. For the Galatian Christians to adopt a Torah-observant lifestyle would mean reintroducing the value of the distinctions that baptism obliterated, over and above the value of shared identity in Christ (DeSilva, 2018, 338). Clearly Paul's focus of the letter is on the tension between Jew and Gentile. In Christ, the Jew (the person of the Law) and the Gentile (the person of the Not-Law), are one. Peter's withdrawal from table fellowship proved contagious precisely along ethnic lines; and that was an event that in Paul's view terminated the Antioch church's witness to the Galatians 3:28 (Martyn, 1997, 243). Their oneness in Christ must be the internalized and displayed signature quality of God's people.

There is neither slave nor free: The second pair is somewhat unexpected because Paul has not mentioned it so far. However, he develops the slave metaphor in 4:1ff. The whole of the letter shows that in writing to the Galatians Paul has no genuine interest in either the second pair of opposites, slave/free (on the social level), or the third, male/female (Martyn, 1997, 380).

Nor is there male and female: As already stated, the third pair may be of secondary relevance alongside "neither Jew nor Gentile." It is highly likely that it refers to Genesis 1:27. "The unity of male and female as equally made in the image of God that is stated in Genesis 1:27 is here reaffirmed as realized in Christ" (Ferguson, 2015). Of course, circumcision as a membership requirement would put women on an inferior level within God's people.

The three couplets have in common that each of them is universally covering all of humanity. Therefore, while Paul focuses on the first, he may have included the second and third for emphasis of the oneness of *all* believers in Christ.

What does "one in Christ Jesus" mean? This is certainly not the only place in which Paul uses the concept of oneness in Christ. See 1 Corinthians 12:25 or Romans 12:4–5. The words παντες (*pantes,* "all"), ὑμεῖς … ἐστὲ (*humeis…este,* "you are"), and ἐν χριστῷ Ἰησοῦ (*en Christo Iesou,* "in Christ Jesus") are all familiar from the thesis statement of verse 26, as the concept of oneness is implied in "all" being "sons of God." There is a new universality of oneness and a new relationship of being God's children (Longenecker, 1990).

Paul does not mean to suggest that Christians no longer have ethnic, social, or sexual identity and differentiation; being "in Christ" does not render Christians androgynous, for instance. Paul does not envisage the identity of Christians to be monolithically identical in matters of this sort. Unity for him does not mean uniformity. Paul perceives Christian unity to involve the coming together of diverse members who are joined despite (or better, because of) their diversity. It is important to recognize that ecclesiastical unity for Paul is not an end in itself nor an anthropological maxim of some sort, as if he thought simply that being associated with others is an obvious good. Instead, the unity of diverse humanity in Christ is a theocentric symbol. It testifies to God's sovereignty in overcoming the forces of chaos that threaten his handiwork. It advertises God's transforming power and over-Lordship in Christ. Christian unity evidences that the high God, who is one and who alone is worthy of worship, is at work in the corporate body of those in Christ (Longenecker, 1998, 66ff). Religious, social, and sexual pairs of opposites are not replaced by equality, but rather by a newly created unity. In Christ (in what Paul will later call "the body of Christ" [1 Corinthians 12:13, 27]), persons who were Jews and persons who were Gentiles have been made into a new unit that is so fundamentally and irreducibly identified with Christ himself as to cause Paul to use the masculine form of the word "one." Members of the church are not one *thing;* they are one *person,* having been taken into the corpus of the One New Man (Martyn, 1997), 377.

Galatians 3:29

> *If you belong to Christ, then you are Abraham's seed, and heirs according to the promise.*

Paul comes back to his thought on Abraham, which he began in 3:7, "Understand, then, that those who have faith are children of Abraham." And what is the promise? The promise is here and now (3:22, 29). If one belongs to Christ, one is presently an heir according to the promise. The verb is in the present tense: you *are* Abraham's seed, and heirs according to the promise. The promise includes the Spirit (3:14). The promise was given to Abraham (3:16, 18) and to Christ (3:16, 19), and is also received by those who belong to Christ (3:22, 29, 4:7). Note how beautifully Galatians 3:29 summarizes the entire passage. The three groups that were to receive the promise—Christ, Abraham, and those who are in Christ—are pulled together: "If you belong to Christ, then you are Abraham's seed, and heirs according to the promise" (Hove, 1999).

Before concluding, we explore four of the bigger theological concepts that are raised in Paul's letter to the Galatians and that are relevant to the interpretation of Galatians 3:26–29. The concepts are "In

Christ," "The New Creation," "The Identity of God's People," and "The Gospel."

Paul's Theology—"In Christ"

The first and probably most important consideration pertains to the language of "in Christ" or "Christ in you." Scholars have long recognized that an examination of "in Christ" can have tremendous implications for understanding Paul's thought (Barcley, 1999). Over one hundred years ago Adolf Deissmann in *Die neutestamentliche Formel "in Christo Jesu"* argued that Paul uses "in Christ" 164 times in his writings (for an overview of the complex history of interpretations of this expression, see Barcley, 1999). This is also one of the main expressions in our passage (ἐν Χριστῷ Ἰησοῦ, *en Christo Iesou* vv. 26, 28), with "baptized into Christ" (εἰς Χριστὸν ἐβαπτίσθητε, *eis Christon ebaptisthate* v. 27) and "[being] of Christ" (Χριστοῦ, *Christou* v. 29) used in synonymous fashion (Longenecker, 1990). In this study, we can only touch on the most significant conclusions for our text.

In a way, to be "in Christ" is a broad and all-encompassing term describing the totality of the believers' existence. "In Christ" includes their allegiance, their identity, their outlook, their ownership, and whose lordship they are under. Paul's conception of "in Christ," however, is broader than simply an intimate, personal communion between the believer and Christ. While Paul speaks of individual believers as being "in Christ," he more consistently applies this expression to the corporate body of believers. This is, of course, the case in Galatians 3:26 and 3:28. Believers "in Christ" have a unity and solidarity with one another because of their common solidarity with Christ (Barcley, 1999). What matters to Paul is not one's race or status or gender. Rather, because of Christ's death, and the participation of the believers through baptism in Christ's death, believers are all united with one another. The "being in Christ" (vv. 26 and 28) is connected with "baptism into Christ" (v. 27), "putting on Christ" (v. 27), and "belonging to Christ" (v. 29). Baptism marks the event in which the believer joins the body of Christ.

The comparison of Galatians 3:27–28 with 1 Corinthians 12:13 and Colossians 3:10–11 shows the consistency of the major motifs: baptism into Christ (or, "one body"), "putting on Christ" (or, "the new man"), listing of two or more pairs of opposites, and the statement that "all" are "one" or that "Christ is all."

A few concluding considerations from this analysis: First and foremost, "in Christ" and "Christ in you" are foundational concepts of Paul's theology. In Galatians they are at the core of Paul's arguments against the false teachers. The indwelling Christ not only provides the basis for transformation to a new life of the believer but also provides a common bond that is the foundation for the unity of the church. Such unity should be visible and transcend all opposites, no matter what they are based on. The term "one in Christ," not the details of the opposites, is the core of Galatians 3:28. (This might be the reason why the parallel passages in 1 Corinthians 12:13 and Colossians 3:10–11 do not list all the opposites: Jew/Gentile, male/female, and slave/free).

Paul's Theology – New Creation

Closely linked to Paul's language of "in Christ" is the idea of a "new creation." In 2 Corinthians 5:17, Paul makes the connection: "If anyone is in Christ, that person (or "there") is a new creation." Paul uses this term for individual converts and for the church, as well as for the cosmos as a whole. In his letter to the Galatians, he uses the term only once and for the church. He writes in 6:15–16: "Neither circumcision nor uncircumcision means anything; what counts is the new creation. Peace and mercy to all who follow this rule—to the Israel of God." Paul equates the church with the "Israel of God." The new creation is a community where "neither circumcision nor uncircumcision is anything." Of course, the three aspects of a new creation intersect. The convert, as part of a community of faith, enters the cosmic drama of re-creation that God inaugurated at the resurrection of Jesus Christ and will bring to completion at the *Parousia* (Hawthorne, Martin and Reid, 1993). The two key characteristics of this community of the new creation are (1) reconciliation and (2) rejection of worldly standards. The Christians are reconciled to God and therefore to one another. One of the greatest witnesses of the church to the world is when peoples once divided are seen to be reconciled to one another in Christ. Such reconciliation can occur only when believers cease living and judging others according to worldly standards. The presence of a new creation means that new standards of unity and peace replace old standards of judgment, prejudice, and divisiveness.

Paul's Theology – The Identity of God's People

This brings us to the next aspect of Paul's theology: the identity of God's people. Galatians 5:13–6:10 has all too often been treated as if it were a mere footnote or appendix to the primary theological concerns of the letter. But in fact, this section is part and parcel of the singular matter that Paul has been addressing all along: the transformed identity of the Christian community (Longenecker, 1998, 81).

The life by the Spirit empowers the Christians to live out the "oneness" in Christ that they are individually and together. The unity must be real in the everyday life of the community. The transformation of the individual must visibly come to life in the one-another relationships. This is the foundation for the "already" of the new creation.

The new creation is the foundation for the new identity of God's people. With the equation of the community of Jews and Gentiles, slaves and free, male and female with the "the Israel of God" (6:16), Paul has eroded the ethnic reference of this term in order to apply it not simply to believing Jews but to Christians whose ethnic heritage may have nothing to do with Jewish parentage. Having identified those in Christ as the offspring of Abraham (3:29, 4:21–31) and the sons of God (4:5–7), it is a short step to identify the church, as he does at the close of his letter, as "the Israel of God" (Longenecker, 1998, 88). This brings to conclusion the discourse concerning Christian identity that Paul began in Galatians 2:15–21. It is key that the law is not to have regulatory force in determining the identity of those in Christ. For Paul, all roads lead to this conclusion.

Paul's Theology – The Gospel

Galatians 4:1–7 does not include the word εὐαγγέλιον (*euangelion*), but it seems obvious that it summarizes well Paul's description of the gospel that is so clearly stated as a main theme in the opening section of the letter (1:6–9, 11, 16). In particular, the statement in verse 4:4 that God sent forth his Son "when the time had fully come" corresponds quite closely to the link in Mark 1:15 between the fulfillment of the time and the preaching of the gospel. The message of the Pauline gospel is this: the true God has sent his Son, in fulfillment of the prophecies of Scripture, to redeem his people from their bondage to false gods; he now sends his own Spirit to make his people truly what they were before only in theory and hope—his own children, heirs of his world (Wright in Jervis and Richardson, 1994). All of this is only possible with Jesus of Nazareth, the crucified and risen one.

This definition of the gospel Paul describes immediately after he has laid out the most important consequence of the gospel for the community of believers: absolute oneness in Christ. "The truth of the gospel" does not allow any of the divisions of Jews and Gentiles to continue in any way—even if performed by the great apostle Peter (Galatians 2:14). The gospel as described here is not simply a doctrinal matter. The gospel concerning Jesus Christ breaks down ethnic barriers and institutes new forms of *koinonia,* fellowship. This is exemplified in Galatians 6:2, where Paul restates the law of Christ as a paradigm of sharing everyday burdens together. The community of believers imitates Jesus' love in how they interact with one another. This is why Peter's failure to share a love-feast together with the Gentiles was such a blatant violation of the gospel. In the end, the letter to the Galatians is Paul's preeminent defense of the gospel.

Conclusion

Galatians 3:28 deserves the recognition and importance that it is often given. Galatians 3:26–29 are at the core of the letter to the Galatians. The importance of the letter in the scope of Paul's theology cannot be overstated. This also means that the letter to the Galatians is a crucial element in God's revelation of his plan of salvation and his Kingdom. This means the stakes couldn't have been higher when Paul— under the guidance of the Holy Spirit—embarked on writing the letter to the Galatians.

Paul is focused on the problem of false teaching in the Galatian churches. There is no other purpose. Paul writes to the Galatians in an atmosphere of discord, both in his own situation and in that of his converts. Concord between the apostle and his converts will be reestablished if he can persuade his audience to ignore or renounce the advice of the agitators and resume following the gospel he had preached when first in Galatia (Witherington III, 1998).

How does he do it? He lays out his arguments carefully, which our overall analysis of the letter touches on. He reminds the Galatians— and us—that the gospel can be "perverted" to the point that it is "no gospel at all." The description of the "truth of the gospel" forms a thread throughout the letter. The gospel replaces the Law as foundation for the identity of the people of God. The new oneness "in Christ" is the foundation of such an identity. The people of God are his sons and daughters, who are united in calling God "Abba." That is possible only through transformation into a new creation that is different from the world but that is also only partially realized on this earth. The foundation of this new creation is Christ: being "in Christ" and "clothed with Christ" and "belonging to Christ" and "one in Christ."

Galatians 3:26–29 is the climax of Paul's argument that began with his report of the Antioch incident (2:11–14). Galatians 3:28 describes God's people in the new covenant. They have been fully associated with Christ; they have been baptized into Christ and have clothed themselves with him. This condition is universal; all are invited to follow, whether Jew or Greek, slave or free, male or female. There is no distinction in God's people: no race, nation, class, or gender has favored status with God. The people of God are the most diverse and at the same time the most united group possible, a people united in God's Son.

So, what are the conclusions with regard to gender-specific roles in the church? Ben Witherington III writes:

> Thus, this text definitely does have social implications for women in Christ. First, it implies they may remain single if they have the χάρισμα to do so. This, in turn, means they can be free to assume roles in the Christian community other than those of wife and mother. They can be free to concentrate wholly on "the things of the Lord" (cf. 1 Corinthians 7:34). Second, it implies sexual, social, and ethnic distinctions cannot be used to determine whether or not one may be or remain in Christ. Third, it implies that such distinctions, while they still exist, should not be used to determine one's standing in Christ, much less to divide the Body of Christ. Baptism into Christ means that one uses one's social, sexual, or ethnic condition to glorify God and build up the Body of Christ. Accordingly, Paul combats a misuse of such distinctions and their relative advantages. Indeed, in the proper context, Paul is willing to argue that there are still advantages to being Jewish (cf. Rom 9:4ff). It is just that these distinctions do not have the significance for one's spiritual status that Paul's opponents seem to be claiming. (Witherington III, 1988, 77)

It seems that this is as far as we can go in drawing conclusions from our text about the situation in the church today. Any further implications from this text on gender-specific roles in the church seem to require a significant "leap" from what Paul wrote.

Galatians 3:28 teaches that we become one in Christ regardless of whether we are Jew/Gentile, male/female, slave/free. However, the passage does not teach that we no longer have any ethnic heritage, gender distinctiveness, or social status in the church.

Bibliography

Barcley, William B. (1999). *Christ in You: A Study in Paul's Theology and Ethics.* University Press of America, Inc, Maryland.

Betz, H.D. (1979). *Galatians. A Commentary on Paul's Letter to the Churches in Galatia.* Fortress Press. Philadelphia.

Das, A.Andrews. (2014). *Galatians.* Concordia Publishing House. St Louis, MO.

DeSilva, D. A. (2018). *The Letter to the Galatians.* William B. Eerdmans Publishing Company, Grand Rapids, MI.

Ferguson, E. (2015). *Women in the Church: Biblical and Historical Perspectives,* Second Edition. Desert Willow Publishing, TX.

Ferguson, S. B. (1986). "The Reformed Doctrine of Sonship." *In Pulpit and People: Essays in Honour of William Still on His 75th Birthday,* eds. Nigel M. de. S. Cameron and Sinclair Ferguson, 81–88. Edinburgh: Rutherford House.

Fung, R.Y.K. "Ministry in the New Testament." In Carson, D.A (1987). *The Church and the Bible and the World.* Baker. Grand Rapids, MI.

Groothuis, R. M. (1997). *Good News for Women: A Biblical Picture of Gender Equality.* Baker. Grand Rapids, MI.

Hawthorne, G., Martin, R.P., and Reid, D. G. (1993). *Dictionary of Paul and his Letters*. InterVarsity Press, IL.

Hove, R. (1999). *Equality in Christ?* Crossway Books, Wheaton, IL.

Jervis, L.A., and Richardson, P. (ed). (1994) *Gospel in Paul. Studies on Corinthians, Galatians and Romans for Richard N. Longenecker.* Sheffield Academic Press Ltd, Sheffield, England.

Kennedy, H.A.A. (1919). *The Theology of the Epistles.* HardPress Publishing. Miami, Fl.

Krimmer, H. (2018). *Galaterbrief.* Edition C Bibelkommentar. Neues Testament. Gerhard Maier (Hrsg.) SCM R. Brockhaus.

Longenecker, R. N. (1990). *Galatians.* Word Biblical Commentary Volume 41. Thomas Nelson Publishers. Nashville.

Longenecker, R. N. (1998). *The Triumph of Abraham's God: The Transformation of Identity in Galatians.* Abingdon Press. Nashville, TN.

Martyn, J. L. (1997). *Galatians.* A New Translation with Introduction and Commentary. The Anchor Yale Bible, Volume 33A. Yale University Press. New Haven & London.

Witherington III, Ben (1988). *Women in the Earliest Churches.* Cambridge University Press. Cambridge, UK.

Witherington III, Ben (1998). *Grace in Galatia—A Commentary on Paul's Letter to the Galatians.* T&T Clark Ltd, Edinburgh, Scotland.

Colossians 3:18–19 & Ephesians 5:21–33

Dr. Brian Perkins
Dr. G. Steve Kinnard

Abstract

The following paper examines and discusses the relevant exegetical issues found in Colossians 3:18–19 and Ephesians 5:21–33 as these passages pertain to the roles of husbands and wives in marriage.

General Introduction to Colossians 3 and Ephesians 5–6

Paul's directives on marriage in Colossians 3 are similar to his directives in Ephesians 5. Many scholars believe that Paul's material in Ephesians 5 is based on Colossians 3. Therefore, we will begin our exegesis with Colossians 3.

A profitable study is a comparison of the household codes in Colossians 3, Ephesians 5–6, and 1 Peter 3. Before you continue with this paper, spend some time looking at these scriptures side by side and note their similarities and differences. By comparing and contrasting the household codes in the New Testament, the reader can begin to see how each code was written to speak to a specific cultural situation, yet the reader can also learn how the codes underscore universal Christian values in relationships.

Greco-Roman Household Code

Paul gives the church his version of household codes in Colossians and Ephesians. These household codes were popular in the Greco-Roman world. Note Aristotle's explanation of household codes in his *Politics:*

> Of household management we have seen that there are three parts —one is the rule of a master over slaves, which has been discussed already, another of a father, and the third of a husband. A husband and father, we saw, rules over wife and children, both free, but the rule differs, the rule over his

children being a royal, over his wife a constitutional rule. For although there may be exceptions to the order of nature, the male is by nature fitter for command than the female, just as the elder and full-grown is superior to the younger and more immature. (Ben Witherington III)

Aristotle's model illustrates the typical Greco-Roman household code of the first century. So questions must be asked: Is Paul simply mimicking other household codes of his day? And if so, is his household code bound by culture or does it transcend culture?

Some scholars believe that since Paul was using the template of household codes as they were used within his culture, the ideas expressed in his codes must be tied to his culture. For example, many Bible readers today do not accept the household code in Ephesians 6 as it applies to slaves obeying their masters as being culturally relevant in the twenty-first century.

So, how should the household codes of Ephesians, Colossians, and 1 Peter be read? Are they descriptive or prescriptive? Are they bound by culture or do they transcend culture? These are sticky exegetical questions.

Perhaps there is a different way to look at the household codes of the New Testament. Perhaps they contain cultural elements and yet transcultural elements at the same time. After all, Paul's directive for husbands to love their wives is categorically different from the directive to husbands in the Greco-Roman household codes where love is never mentioned. Paul also uses Jesus as his standard of love and behavior in his codes. Does anyone want to say that Paul's admonition for husbands to "love your wives, just as Christ also loved the church and gave himself up for her" was only for the first century and is not applicable today? And, Paul directs comments to the traditional power holder in his household codes. This was not typically done. Ben Witherington III writes,

Non-Christian household codes almost always direct exhortations only to the subordinate members of the household. What is new about the code here then is the Christian limitations placed on the head of household. That is what would stand out to an ancient person hearing Paul's discourse for the first time. (Witherington III, 187)

Paul takes the household code and "Christianizes" it. In doing so, he speaks to his culture and to all cultures.

Paul was working in the culture of his day. His ideas were subversive to the current norms of his day; however, they fell short of calling for an open revolution. Paul's ideas of a husband loving his wife, a father not exasperating his children, and all disciples submitting to one another out of reverence for Christ were subversive. Paul did not adhere to the Greco-Roman household codes; instead, he modified them under the standard of King Jesus. So, let's be careful not to throw away these valuable parts of Scripture just because they do not mesh well with our twenty-first-century Western values. Perhaps our values need to be reevaluated in light of Colossians 3 and Ephesians 5–6.

Colossians 3:18–19

Introduction to Colossians 3:18–19

In Colossians, Paul is writing to a group of Christians that he has not met personally. He has concerns about their spiritual growth. He presents Christ to them and seeks to help them mature in Christ apart from rules and regulations. He wants them to live as people who have been made alive in Christ. He gives them directives for living together in community and focuses them on prayer and maturity before giving final directions.

Paul placed the passage under consideration in a section on how Christians should live together in community. Three pairs of relationships are discussion in this section: husbands-wives, parents-children, masters-slaves.

The attitude toward family in Colossae at the time of this writing was similar to that in Ephesus. The husband/father was viewed as the authority over the household, and wives and children were seen as property. As Paul wrote to the churches in Colossae, the "new Roman woman" was making her way into that city and the rest of Asia Minor (Bruce W. Winter, *Romans Wives, Roman Widows*). She was an independent woman who did not wish to adhere to the social norms of the Greco-Roman world. Perhaps Paul is specifically writing to the church in Colossae to alert the disciples of Jesus as to how to live differently from the standards of Roman society so that they would shine like a light in a dark world. However, it is difficult to know the exact *sitz im leben* of the church in Colossae. Caution should always be applied when basing interpretation on first-century historical context. The context should be considered, but not overvalued.

The Text of Colossians 3:18–19

Colossians 3:18–19 (UBS Greek Text, 5th Edition)

[18] Αἱ γυναῖκες, ὑποτάσσεσθε τοῖς ἀνδράσιν ὡς ἀνῆκεν ἐν κυρίῳ.
[19] Οἱ ἄνδρες, ἀγαπᾶτε τὰς γυναῖκας καὶ μὴ πικραίνεσθε πρὸς αὐτάς.

Colossians 3:18–19 (NASB 1995)

[18]*Wives, be subject to your husbands, as is fitting in the Lord.*
[18]*Husbands, love your wives and do not be embittered against them.*

Colossians 3:18–19 (NIV 2011)

[18]*Wives, submit yourselves to your husbands, as is fitting in the Lord.*
[18]*Husbands, love your wives and do not be harsh with them.*

Verses 18 and 19 are closely connected with each other. Both give directives for partners in marriage. Both contain verbs that are in the imperative mood in the Greek (commands). Verse 18 contains one command for the wives—submit to your husbands. Verse 19 contains two commands for the husbands—love your wives and do not be embittered against your wives.

Direction to Wives in Colossians 3:18

In verse 18, there is no doubt what the verb is (as compared to Ephesians 5:22, where the verb must be supplied by the translator). The verb is ὑποτάσσεσθε (*hypotassesthe*, "submit, subordinate"). It is a present middle and/or passive imperative of ὑποτάσσω (*hypotassō*, "to cause to be in a submissive relationship, to subject, to subordinate," BDAG). The middle voice denotes that the subject is acting upon itself. The verse can be translated as "Wives, you submit yourselves to the husbands as is proper in the Lord." Murray J. Harris writes, "It is a case of voluntary submission in recognition of the God-appointed leadership of the husband and the divinely ordained hierarchical order in creation (cf. 1 Corinthians 11:3–9; Ephesians 5:22–24)" (Harris, 155). Some might bristle at the use of the word "hierarchical," but the Bible teaches that hierarchies exist. Some are benevolent, others are benign, and others are abusive.

The use of the word ὑποτάσσω (*hypotassō*, "to submit") does not imply that the husband is of greater value than the wife. The role of husband and the role of wife are equally valued ones. Regarding the word "submit," Ben Witherington III notes that it "surely does not imply the ontological inferiority of the submitter to the one submitted to. Rather it has to do with the nature of a relationship between two persons. It may also in fact have more to do with following the example of Christ, who humbled himself and took a lower place" (Witherington III, 190).

The phrase "as is proper" is ὡς ἀνῆκεν (*hos anaken,* from the verb ἀνήκω, *anékō*), meaning, "it belongs, it is fit, proper, or becoming" (BDAG). It is the imperfect tense of the verb and could be translated, "as was fitting in the Lord," which implies that this is the typical Christian practice (a habitual imperfect). Wives are to submit to their husbands as is proper, right, and fitting in the Lord. This suggests that it is improper or unfitting for a wife to be anything other than submissive to her husband.

The phrase "as is fitting in the Lord" can mean that this is a duty born out of the wife's discipleship to Jesus. Harris writes, "The Lord (Jesus) is the yardstick for determining what is fitting (v. 18) or pleasing (v. 20)" (Harris, 155). The wife voluntarily submits herself to the leadership of her husband out of her loving commitment to him and her devotion to Jesus.

Another view says that "as is fitting" effectively limits the wife to submit in such a way that honors Jesus and permits her not to submit if her husband's leadership directs her to do something contrary to the will of God, for example, to sin. This second view is supported by passages that direct us to obey God rather than human beings (Acts 5:29) and to love God above all else (Luke 14). However, this meaning is less likely based on the Greek syntax.

Direction to Husbands in Colossians 3:19

The husband must love his wife, but Paul adds that the husband must not be embittered against his wife. Embittered here is πικραίνεσθε (*pikrainesthe*). It is the present passive imperative of πικραίνω (*pikrainō*), meaning, "to be enraged, angry, or incensed" (BDAG). Husbands are to love their wives but not become angry or bitter toward them. Husbands must not treat their wives harshly. They must avoid all bitterness toward their wives. This would include both their words and actions. This implies more than acting out of a sense of duty; instead, the husband works to keep a soft heart, one that does not grow bitter toward his wife.

This added direction to the husband implies that some husbands found it difficult to love their wives without a sense of regret or irritation, which when left unchecked led to bitterness, resentment, and hostility. These attitudes are improper for God's holy people (Ephesians 4:31) and are unacceptable in marriage. The love a husband has for his wife should therefore be unforced and sincere.

When a husband loves his wife, he creates an environment where the wife willingly submits to his love. Their relationship becomes a partnership, a dance of love and willing submission that honors Jesus.

Ephesians 5:21–33

Introduction to Ephesians 5:21–33

Ephesians is a general letter written in two main sections. Chapters 1–3 are more theologically focused, and chapters 4–6 are more practically focused. The first section explains that God's holy people have every blessing in Christ, have been made alive in Christ, and have been united in Christ. The second section explains how God's holy people should be unified and should mature in Christ, and how God's holy people should live individually, relationally, and spiritually. The passage under consideration appears in the second section, where Paul explains how we should live in relation to others as a direct result of being filled with the Spirit (5:18). In every relationship there should be submission to one another out of a holy respect for Christ (5:21).

The Setting of Ephesians

The general attitude toward family in Ephesus at the time of Paul's writing was that the husband led the family with absolute authority, and the wife and children were understood to be the husband's possessions (Marshall, 2004).

During the time of Paul, Ephesus was the fourth largest city in the world, with a population of 250,000 people. It was the leading city in the province of Asia. At the center of cultic life in Ephesus was the Temple of Artemis. Women priestesses oversaw the worship of the Artemis shrine. This empowered some of the women in Ephesus to be independent and live outside the general social norms of Greco-Roman society. Exactly how large this segment of the female population was during the first century is debated (see Baugh).

Also, walking onto the scene in Ephesus (and other cities in the East) was the "new Roman woman." She was an independent woman who had no desire to submit to her husband or follow the social mores of the Roman Empire. She did not see herself as the property of any man, and she wasn't afraid to express her freedom in public.

Perhaps some of what Paul wrote in his letter to the Ephesians came from his desire to squelch the influence of the Artemis priestesses and the "new Roman woman." It is difficult to paint a perfect picture of the cultural backdrop for the Letter to the Ephesians because new archaeological discoveries continue to bring new evidence to light that must be evaluated. These are sticky exegetical issues. The reader must be careful not to base exegesis too heavily on a reconstructed sociological model of ancient Ephesus. The reader would be wise to ascertain the lasting Christian values Paul communicates to the members of the church in Ephesus by focusing on what Paul said in his letter.

The church in Ephesus was started near the end of Paul's second missionary journey around AD 52. The letter was written during Paul's imprisonment about AD 61.

Text of Ephesians 5:21–33

Ephesians 5:21–33 (NASB 1995)

²¹*and be subject to one another in the fear of Christ.*

²²*Wives, be subject to your own husbands, as to the Lord.*

²³*For the husband is the head of the wife, as Christ also is the head of the church, He Himself being the Savior of the body.*

²⁴*But as the church is subject to Christ, so also the wives* ought to be *to their husbands in everything.*

²⁵*Husbands, love your wives, just as Christ also loved the church and gave*

Himself up for her,

²⁶so that He might sanctify her, having cleansed her by the washing of water with the word,

²⁷that He might present to Himself the church in all her glory, having no spot or wrinkle or any such thing; but that she would be holy and blameless.

²⁸So husbands ought also to love their own wives as their own bodies. He who loves his own wife loves himself;

²⁹for no one ever hated his own flesh, but nourishes and cherishes it, just as Christ also does the church,

³⁰because we are members of His body.

³¹For this reason a man shall leave his father and mother and shall be joined to his wife, and the two shall become one flesh.

³²This mystery is great; but I am speaking with reference to Christ and the church.

³³Nevertheless, each individual among you also is to love his own wife even as himself, and the wife must see to it that she respects her husband.

Ephesians 5:21–33 (NIV 2011)

²¹Submit to one another out of reverence for Christ.

²²Wives, submit yourselves to your own husbands as you do to the Lord. ²³For the husband is the head of the wife as Christ is the head of the church, his body, of which he is the Savior. ²⁴Now as the church submits to Christ, so also wives should submit to their husbands in everything.

²⁵Husbands, love your wives, just as Christ loved the church and gave himself up for her ²⁶to make her holy, cleansing her by the washing with water through the word, ²⁷and to present her to himself as a radiant church, without stain or wrinkle or any other blemish, but holy and blameless. ²⁸In this same way, husbands ought to love their wives as their own bodies. He who loves his wife loves himself. ²⁹After all, no one ever hated their own body, but they feed and care for their body, just as Christ does the church—³⁰for we are members of his body. ³¹"For this reason a man will leave his father and mother and be united to his wife, and the two will become one flesh." ³²This is a profound mystery—but I am talking about Christ and the church. ³³However, each one of you also must love his wife as he loves himself, and the wife must respect her husband.

Overview of Ephesians 5:21–33

Ephesians 5:21–33 can be divided into four parts. The first verse (v. 21) lays out the universal premise of mutual submission. The second section (vv. 22–24) addresses wives. The third section (vv. 25–32) addresses husbands. The final verse (v. 33) is a summary of the passage. Both sections that address spouses start out with a premise of submission or love and then move on to explain why this attitude is commanded. This passage clearly shows a difference of roles in the marriage between the husband and the wife.

Although it is outside the scope of this paper, it should not be overlooked that the discussion of household codes does not end at 5:33. Instead, the discussion continues into chapter six with a focus on children, parents, slaves, and masters. Exegetes need to be consistent when interpreting this passage. If they determine that Paul has nothing to say to slaves and masters today or that Paul's comments to slaves and masters in 6:15–19 are culturally cloaked, they must be consistent and apply the same view toward the relationship between wives and husbands in 5:21–33.

However, although Paul was clearly working toward the liberation of all humanity in his letters, he acknowledged the fact of slavery as an institution in his context. Therefore, in 6:15–19 Paul gave codes of conduct for Christian slaves and masters in the "already, but not yet" of the kingdom of King Jesus. This unrealized eschatology is an important concept to consider in exegesis. We need to appreciate the "ideal" of what will be realized in heaven versus what is inaugurated, unrealized, "already, but not yet," in this present age. Jesus inaugurated this new age, which will be fully realized when he comes.

Paul did have something to say to Christian slaves and masters within the first-century context. In the same way, he also has something to say to Christian wives and husbands, and parents and children, within that same context. How this applies to people outside the first-century context is a more difficult question to answer. That is the million-dollar exegetical question: What is cultural and is meant to be applied to the first-century church, and what is transcultural and is meant to be applied to all culture throughout history?

Ephesians 5:21 – The Mutual Submission Umbrella

Mutual submission out of reverence for Christ is expected of all followers of Jesus. Paul begins the conversation on relationships here. Everything that he says after this opening statement falls under this umbrella of submitting to one another out of reverence for Christ.

No disciple has the advantage of "free reign" in how they are to treat another disciple. Verse 21 contains the participle ὑποτασσόμενοι (*hypotassomenoi,* "being subject to"), which refers back to the main verb in verse 18, "be filled" (πληροῦσθε, *plērousthe,* from πληρόω, *plēroō,* "to be filled"). Submission, then, is one of four responses that characterize, in general, what a Spirit-filled life in Christ looks like (O'Brien, 1999). A Spirit-filled life is characterized by:

(1) Speaking to one another with psalms, hymns and spiritual songs.

(2) Singing and making music in your heart to the Lord.

(3) Giving thanks to God for everything.

(4) Submitting to one another out of reverence for Christ.

When verse 21 is used as a conclusion to the preceding passage (vv. 15–20), it is seen as a general directive. But other exegetes have narrowed the application. Boles (1993) says that the actual command to submit is directed only to the first of the three separate pairs mentioned in the text: wives to husbands, children to parents, and slaves to masters. However, it seems best to take this principle as an overarching principle that applies in general to everyone, but is exercised uniquely for every person in the three pairs mentioned based on the directives given (Knight, 1991), (Padgett, 2011). In other words, it applies generally to every disciple, but it also serves as an introduction to the household code that follows. Thus, every disciple lives under the umbrella of submitting to one another.

It should also be noted that the admonition to "submit to one another" does not negate the differences in roles and leadership positions that exist within the church and in marriage. The idea of mutual submission does not negate apostolic authority or the authority of elders in the church. Lincoln in his commentary on Ephesians writes,

There is an interesting parallel in 1 Peter 5:5 where the exhortation "you that are younger be subject to the elders" is followed immediately by the further appeal "clothe yourselves, all of you, with humility toward one another." The latter admonition was not meant to cancel out the former. Rather, the writer holds that there is a general sense in which elders are to serve their flock, including its younger element, in a submissive attitude, but that mutuality goes along with a hierarchical view of roles. (Lincoln, *Ephesians*, 366)

Paul's umbrella of "submit to one another" does not negate the admonition that wives are to submit to their husbands and husbands are to love their wives. Differential aspects in roles in marriage ought to be valued.

Direction to Wives in Ephesians 5:22–24

First, it is best to give a literal translation of verse 22. The Greek text reads, "αἱ γυναῖκες τοῖς ἰδίοις ἀνδράσιν ὡς τῷ κυρίῳ," which when translated literally reads, "the wives to their own husbands as to the Lord." The word ὑποτασσόμενοι (*hyotassomenoi*, "submit") is not found in verse 22. However, the verse begs for a verb, and the closest verb to the verse is actually the participle that serves as an umbrella for the passage in verse 21 (ὑποτασσόμενοι, *hyotassomenoi*, "submit"). Therefore, the verse is normally translated as, "Wives submit to their own husbands as to the Lord."

This wording is quite different from the direction given to children and slaves, who are called to simply obey (ὑπακούετε, *hupakoúete*). The word ὑποτάσσω (*hupotássō*) means, "to subject or to subordinate" (BDAG). It is used in the middle voice in this passage. This can signify an action that someone does to oneself, thus, "Wives you submit yourselves to your own husbands." Submission here is not being subordinated under another person by force. Rather it is a voluntary yielding of oneself to another. In this context this is done in love (Knight, 1991). This dynamic is a characteristic of the Christian faith and is highlighted by Paul in Philippians 2:3 as an action Christians undertake in order to imitate Christ (Philippians 2:5; see also Matthew 20:26–28). This same term is used in the relation of a wife to her husband in Colossians 3:18; 1 Peter 3:1, 5; and Titus 2:5. A wife is called to willingly submit herself to her husband as she would submit herself to Christ. This directive is a responsibility she has as a wife. It also falls under the umbrella of every Christian submitting themselves to every other Christian out of reverence for Christ, as seen in 5:21.

Paul goes on in verse 23 to spell out the reason for this directive to wives. He writes that the husband is the head of the wife just as Jesus is the head of the church. The word used for head is (κεφαλή, *kephalē*), which literally means "head or top," but metaphorically means "the leader, source, chief, or one to whom others are subordinate" (BDAG).

Kephalē is used metaphorically in this passage, and this has led scholars to interpret this word in one of two ways.

Kephalē Examined

First, much has been written to support the view that *kephalē* here means "source" or "origin" (Kroeger, 1993), (Padgett, 2011), (Mickelson, 1986), (Payne, 2009). If this view is accepted, then the husband is not the head of the wife as the authoritative head, but he is the "source" or "origin" of the wife.

Supporters of this view note the following:

1. They point to other metaphorical uses of *kephalē* (1 Corinthians 11:3; Colossians 2:19; Ephesians 4:15–16), which reads better as "source" or "origin." This is stated as proof that *kephalē* should not always mean "head" or "authority."

2. They prefer the Lidell & Scott lexicon to Bauer's lexicon because it does not give "authority" as a translation for *kephalē*.

3. The Septuagint translated the same metaphor of head as leader/ authority using a different word (*archon*) 109 times compared to *kephalē* 9 times.

4. In Ephesians 5:21–33, Jesus is the head of the church by taking care of her, not by lording it over her.

5. "Submit to one another" in verse 21 virtually reduces the direction for the husband in verse 22 to mutual submission.

6. Spiritual leadership in the Bible is always presented as servant leadership, not as hierarchal or authoritarian leadership.

7. The admonition for a husband to submit, while not explicitly stated, is implicit in verses 21, 25, 28, and 33.

Second, there are others who support the view that *kephalē* here means, "head, leader, or one bearing authority" (Marshal, 2004), (Knight, 1991), (Grudem, 2002 & 1991), (Tucker, 1986). This view states that "headship" implies authority. Wayne Grudem is a major advocate of this view. He states that *kephalē* can mean "authority over" (Piper & Grudem, Appendix 1).

However, it is possible for someone to hold this position of "headship" and maintain that marriage works as a partnership where both partners have equal input and both partners work together for the benefit of the marriage. Even if *kephalē* means "authority over," one still has to look at the type of authority described in the passage, i.e., the authority of Jesus, who came as a servant.

Supporters of this viewpoint state the following:

1. The wife is called to submit to her husband as to the Lord (v. 22). This is authoritative.

2. Christ is the head of the church (v. 23) and exercises authority over her (Ephesians 1:22), so the husband, as head, must also be recognized as the authority over his wife.

3. The wife is called to submit to her husband in everything. This is absolute. This directive is consistently taught in Scripture (Ephesians 5:22; Colossians 3:18; 1 Peter 3:1; Titus 2:4).

4. The focus throughout this passage is one of submission, especially of the wife to her husband as her head (vv. 22–24).

5. The other uses of *kephalē* in Ephesians are more aligned to "authority" or "first in rank" versus "source."

6. The evidence to support that *kephalē* means "source" is weak and unpersuasive. Wayne Grudem has found that there are only two examples from ancient literature that support this view (and both are inconclusive). The evidence to support *kephalē* as "authority over" is substantial. Forty-nine specific ancient texts have been cited. (Piper & Grudem, Appendix 1)

The following discussion makes a case as to which view seems most in keeping with Paul's intent. This is the view that *kephalē* is best translated as head, but this "headship" must reflect the attitude of Jesus.

1. After a careful review of verses 23–24, it can be shown that a chiasm was used by Paul in this discussion. *Chiasms* are often employed to give emphasis in prose. This *chiasm* emphasizes the relationship between Jesus and the church.

> For the husband is the head of
>> the wife,
>>> as Christ also is the head of
>>>> the church,
>>>>> **he himself *being* the Savior of the body.**
>>>> But as the church is subject
>>> to Christ, so also
>> the wives *ought to be*
> to their husbands in everything.

Christ's relationship and service to the church models the husband's relationship and service to his wife. The wife should willingly submit herself to her husband as the church willingly submits to Christ.

2. This pattern of wives submitting to their husbands is established outside of Paul's writing. See Peter's statement in 1 Peter 3:1.

3. The most telling reason to think of *kephalē* as "benevolent authority" in verse 23 is because of the parallel Paul establishes in the verses that follow between the husband and wife and Christ and the church. Here is the parallel:

> [23]*"For the husband is the head of the wife, as Christ also is the head of the church."*

The parallels in the analogy continue as follows:

> [23]*"For the husband is the head of the wife as Christ is the head of the church, his body, of which he is the Savior."*

> [28]*"So husbands ought also to love their own wives as their own bodies. He who loves his own wife loves himself; [29]for no one ever hated his own*

flesh, but nourishes and cherishes it, just as Christ also does *the church,* *³⁰because we are members of His body."*

Paul moves in his analogy from the husband and Christ being the head, to the wife and the church being the body. The second part of the analogy where the husband cares for the wife as Christ cares for the church is lost when "head" is thought of as "source" as in "the source or origin of a river." If Paul had wanted the analogy to be the image of a river, he could easily have used that illustration. However, he uses the image of a human body. The *kephalḗ* is the head of the body.

Plus, Paul is clear that the church submits to the "headship" of Christ. And he is clear that the wife submits to her husband. He writes, "Now as the church submits to Christ, so also wives should submit to their husbands in everything." Paul establishes this parallel. As the church submits to Christ, a wife submits to her husband.

4. The other uses of headship in Paul's writings are consistent with the view that *kephalḗ* means "authority."

The reference to the headship of Jesus over the church is used in 1 Corinthians 11:3; Ephesians 1:22, 4:15; and Colossians 1:18. The passages in Ephesians illuminate the meaning of "headship." For example:

- Ephesians 1:22 – "And God placed (*hupotássō*) all things under his feet and appointed him to be head (*kephalḗ*) over everything for the church." (NIV 2011)

God has placed all things (v. 21, "all rule and authority, power and dominion, and every name that is invoked, both the present age and in the one to come") under Jesus' feet. This means that Jesus has authority over everything (Matthew 28:18) including the church. Thus the church submits to the headship of Jesus (Dawes, 1998). Boles (1993) agrees that Paul's usage of headship in Ephesians 1:22 is conclusive in supporting the idea of "head" or "leader" in Ephesians 5.

- Ephesians 4:15 – "Instead, speaking the truth in love, we will grow to become in every respect the mature body of him who is the head (*kephalḗ*), that is, Christ." (NIV 2011)

As the head of the church, Jesus is the model the church seeks to emulate. The church is to follow his example. Richards (1991) says that in marriage, headship emphasizes the husband's Christlike role of sustaining and protecting his wife as well as encouraging her personal and spiritual growth. In marriage, the husband is to mirror the attitude and actions of Jesus with the church.

Direction to Husbands in Ephesians 5:25–32

Next, Paul addresses the husband directly. His direct appeal to the husband is not paralleled in the Hebrew Bible or in Greco-Roman household codes. Also, Paul uses 116 words to admonish the husband and only 41 words to give directives to the wife (Hoehner, 746, 748). The way that Paul gives direction to the person who would have been seen as the power broker in the household code was unique to Paul and was one of the ways he "Christianized" the household codes.

Husbands (v. 25) are to love their wives just as Christ loved the church and gave himself up for her. Paul draws another parallel here. As Christ is to the church, the husband is to be to his wife. Note that this directive does not allow the husband to be domineering or excessive in his use of authority in the relationship. In fact, the path of the love of Christ is the way of submission, subordination, self-sacrifice, humility, and servant leadership. There is no hint of oppressive patriarchy or domineering hierarchy in the way a husband relates to his wife, because he loves her with *agape* love just like Christ loves the church.

Paul explains in verses 26–27 how Jesus loved the church. This helps define what he means by "love your wives." Jesus made the church holy, set it apart for himself, and cleansed it by the power of the Word. Jesus sanctified the church to present it to himself as glorious, not having any type of stain, wrinkle, or blemish, but he presented it as holy and blameless. This is a restatement of the spiritual blessings we have in Christ as stated in Ephesians 1:4. Jesus used his role as the head of the church to make it radiant, not to control it.

In this exact way, husbands are obligated to love their wives as they love their own bodies. Loving your wife is the same as loving yourself. Paul says that no one hates his own body, but nourishes and cherishes it. Jesus also nourishes and nurtures the church.

This directive to the husband would have been a shocking change from what was the typical expectation of marriage in Paul's time. In general, a wife was considered to be her husband's property. Common Greco-Roman household codes do not expect a husband to lay down his life for his wife's welfare. This does not mean that husbands did not love their wives; it only suggests that sacrificial love was not an expectation in marriage in Greco-Roman society. Jesus changed all that for his people. In the Christian culture husbands were to consider the needs of their wives above their own. In this way, husbands needed to learn submission. The husband's needs no longer came first. He had to submit his desires and wants to his wife's desires, and thus demonstrate *agape* love. This is exemplified in the partnership in ministry of Aquila and Priscilla in Acts 18:18–26; Romans 16:3–5; 1 Corinthians 16:19; and 2 Timothy 4:19.

In verse 31, Paul references Genesis 2:24 as a source for understanding the one-body concept. This scripture says that in marriage the husband and the wife become one flesh, or one body. How this happens is a mystery, but it is echoed by the many members forming one body in the church.

Paul's Summary in Ephesians 5:33

> *However, each one of you also must love his wife as he loves himself, and the wife must respect her husband. (NIV 2011)*

In verse 33, Paul concludes his discussion on marriage. The marriage relationship must be one of love and respect. The husband must love and care for his wife as he lovingly cares for his own body, and the wife must respect and submit to her husband. The primary beneficiary of each command is the other spouse. The husband benefits when the wife submits to him, and the wife benefits when the husband loves her. Thus, each role in marriage fulfills the direction to submit to one another out of reverence for Christ.

Paul began his argument in verse 21 with the word φόβος (*phobos*, "fear, respect"), and he ends his argument in verse 33 with the same word in its verb form (φοβέω, *phobeō*, "fear, respect"). In verse 21, disciples of Jesus must submit to one another out of "fear, respect" for Christ. In verse 33, the wife is to "fear, respect" her husband. Paul's symmetry is difficult to miss. In fact it is quite beautiful. Respect toward a spouse begins with respect for Jesus. Respect for Jesus ends with respect toward others, especially toward a spouse.

Conclusions

1. Paul introduces his discussion of marriage and the other household codes with a general principle and an overarching directive—disciples of Jesus must "submit to one another out of reverence for Christ" (Ephesians 5:21).

2. The wife is called to submit to her husband as is proper in the Lord.

3. The husband is called to love his wife and be careful to watch his heart lest he become bitter.

4. Husbands serve as the head of their wife just as Jesus is the head of the church.

5. Husbands are directed to love their wives as Jesus loves the church.

6. These directives are not dependent on the obedience of the spouse.

7. Each partner in a marriage plays a role that mirrors the relationship between Jesus and the church.

Reflections

The aim of these directives from Paul is to help followers of Jesus to be more like Jesus (Ephesians 5:1). Marriage is meant to be a reflection of the relationship between Jesus and the church. The roles in marriage were not to imitate the patriarchy that was common in Roman society, but to transform marriage into the ideals of the Kingdom of God.

The following thoughts are given to help apply these concepts to our culture today.

Submit to One Another

"Submitting to one another" is the umbrella under which all relationships in Jesus find shelter from the rain and shade from the sun.

We see an example of submitting to one another in the relationship between God the Father and God the Son. In working together, the Father and Son know each other (Matthew 11:26; John 7:29, 8:55, 10:15), love each other (John 3:35, 5:20, 14:31), and glorify each other (John 17:1, 4–5). As the authority, the Father sent the Son (Galatians 4:4; 1 John 4:14; Romans 8:3) and directed him (Mark 12:36). In submission, the Son does what the Father does (John 5:19), seeks to please him (John 5:30), speaks for him (John 7:16, 8:28, 12:49–50, 14:10, 24), and makes the Father known (John 17:26). This was done to bring salvation to humankind. All the while Jesus was one with the Father (John 10:30, 17:22) and was no less than the Father (John 14:9; Hebrews 1:3). Jesus is a person in the Godhead along with the Father (Matthew 28:19–20; 2 Corinthians 13:14), but he willingly submitted himself (Philippians 2:6–7) to the Father's direction for our benefit (Matthew 26:42).

The relationship between God the Father and God the Son offers an excellent example of mutual submission among coequal partners who work for the same goal. Followers of Jesus submit to one another out of reverence for Christ. This submission to one another allows us to work together as partners for the glory of God.

In marriage, both partners work together. The loving husband works to benefit his wife as he loves his wife as Christ loves the church. The husband loves his wife by valuing her as a person. He values her opinion and makes decisions that are based on her input and for her welfare. The wife respectfully gives her thoughts and contributes her opinion to her husband with the understanding that he leads her with benevolent authority.

Wives, Submit to Your Husbands

Perhaps a good example to help us understand the submission of the wife to the husband is the example of how the church follows Jesus for the purpose of world evangelism. Jesus is the head of the church. The church submits to Jesus and works together with him for a common purpose—the salvation of many. Jesus has given the church the direction, the encouragement, and the commandment—go make disciples. He has demonstrated his love and care for the church by giving her the Holy Spirit as a guide. The church submits by sharing the good news of the Kingdom with others. While Jesus is the head the church, the church has much freedom. Jesus does not force or coerce the church to follow, but he motivates through his own love and self-sacrifice. The church willingly follows Jesus as its head.

As Christ is head of the church, the husband is head of the wife. As the church follows the sacrificial servant leadership of Jesus, the wife does the same with her husband.

The journey of marriage follows a path of agreement and disagreement. Devoted spouses learn to walk through the landmines of disagreement by loving each other and by learning to make concessions with each another. A loving husband will understand that he is not right all the time, and he will value the input of his wife in areas where he is weak. At the same time, a loving wife will recognize that she can disagree with her husband without being disagreeable. This is the beautiful dance called marriage.

Husbands, Love your Wives

Paul continues his analogy by saying that as Christ loved the church and gave himself for her, so the husband ought to love his wife. The love of a husband for his wife ought to be characterized by self-sacrifice, putting the needs of the wife above his own and being vigilant to meet her needs. That is the love Christ has for the church.

The actions taken by the husband must be motivated out of love and by what is most beneficial for everyone involved. The headship of the husband is not a license for self-centeredness, a hunger for power, domineering control, or abusive behavior. Quite the opposite. As the head, the husband must be willing to suffer and lay down his life for the spiritual health of his wife. The husband does not always get his way. In fact, a godly husband will give up his selfish desires for the good of his wife. If an intended action only benefits him, then he will not choose that action. The standard of the husband loving the wife as Christ loved the church is an impossibly high standard. It can only be achieved by God's grace.

God's grace. That's the perfect place to end this paper. It is only by God's grace that husbands and wives can be who they need to be in marriage. Thanks be to the God of all grace.

Bibliography

Bauer, Walter, Arndt, W. F., and Gingrich, F. W., *A Greek-English Lexicon of the New Testament,* revised by F. W. Danker, 3rd ed. (Chicago: University of Chicago Press, 2000).

Baugh, S. M. "Cult Prostitution in New Testament Ephesus: A Reappraisal." *Journal of the Evangelical Theological Society.* 42.3 (1999): 443–460.

Boles, K. L. (1993). *Galatians & Ephesians.* (Ephesians 5:22). Joplin, MO: College Press.

Dawes, G. W. (1998). *The Body in Question: Metaphor and Meaning in the Interpretation of Ephesians 5:21–33,* 139–142. Leiden, Boston: Brill.

Grudem, Wayne (1991). "The Meaning of Kephalē ("Head"): A Response to Recent Studies." In John Piper & Wayne Grudem, *Recovering Biblical Manhood & Womanhood,* 425–468. Wheaton, IL: Crossway Books.

_____ (2002). "The Meaning of κεφαλή ("Head"): An Evaluation of New Evidence, Real and Alleged." In W. A. Grudem (Ed.), *Biblical Foundations for Manhood and Womanhood,* 146–202. Wheaton, IL: Crossway Books.

Harris, Murray J. *Colossians and Philemon. Exegetical Guide to the Greek New Testament.* (Nashville: B&H Academic, 2013), 154.

H. Hoehner, H. *Ephesians* (Grand Rapids: Baker, 2002).

Kinnard, G. Steve. *Jesus Unequaled: An Exposition of Colossians.* (Spring, TX: Illumination Publishers, 2013).

Knight, George W. (1991). "Husbands and Wives as Analogues of Christ and the Church: Ephesians 5:21–33 and Colossians 3:18–19." In John Piper and Wayne Grudem, *Recovering Biblical Manhood & Womanhood.* Crossway Books, Wheaton, IL, 165–178.

Kroeger, Catherine. (1993) "Head." *Dictionary of Paul and His Letters.* (375–377) Downers Grove, IL and Leicester, England: InterVarsity.

Lincoln, A. T., *Ephesians,* WBC 42. (Waco: Word, 1990).

Marshall, Howard I. (2004) "Mutual Love and Submission in Marriage: Colossians 3:18–19 and Ephesians 5:21–33," 186–204. In Ronald

Pierce and Rebecca Merrill Groothuis, *Discovering Biblical Equality: Complementarity without Hierarchy,* Downers Grove, IL: Intervarsity Press.

Mickelson Alvera & Berkeley. (1986) "What does Kephale mean in the New Testament," 95–117) in *Women, Authority & the Bible.* Intervarsity Press, Downers Grove, Il

O'Brien, P. T. (1999). *The Letter to the Ephesians,* 399. Grand Rapids, MI: W.B. Eerdmans Publishing Co.

Padgett, Alan (2011). *As Christ Submit to the Church: A Biblical Understanding of Leadership and Mutual Submission,* 57-77. Grand Rapids, MI: Baker Publishing.

Payne, Philip B. (2009) *Man and Woman, One in Christ: An Exegetical and Theological Study of Paul's Letters,* 271–290). Grand Rapids, MI: Zondervan.

Richards, L. O. (1991). *The Bible Reader's Companion* (electronic ed.), 802. Wheaton: Victor Books.

Tucker, Ruth A. Response to "What does Kephale mean in the New Testament," *Women, Authority & the Bible.* Intervarsity Press, Downers Grove, Il, 95–117

Walker, William O. (1983) "The Theology of Woman's Place and the Paulist Tradition," 287–300, *Paul and His Legacy.* Salem, Oregon: Polebridge Press

Wilson, Dr. Ralph F. (1975), Headship (*kephalē*) and Submission (*hupotassomai*) in Ephesians 5:21–33. This is a paper submitted to Dr. Norman Wakefield, Fuller Theological Seminary, December 4, 1975.

Winter, Bruce W. *Romans Wives, Roman Widows* (Grand Rapids, MI: Wm. B. Eerdmans Publishing Co., 2007), 2003.

Witherington III, Ben. *The Letters to Philemon, the Colossians, and the Ephesians: A Socio-Rhetorical Commentary on the Captivity Epistles.* (Grand Rapids, MI: Wm. B. Eerdmans Publishing Co., 2007).

Wright, N. T. *Colossians and Philemon* (Grand Rapids: Eerdmans, 1986).

Zodhiates, S. (2000). *The Complete Word Study Dictionary: New Testament* (electronic ed.). Chattanooga, TN: AMG Publishers.

CHAPTER SIX

1 Timothy 2:8–15

Dr. G. Steve Kinnard, Dr. Glenn Giles,
Valdur Koha, Suzette Lewis, Kay McKean,
Dr. Gregg Marutzky, Jeanie Shaw

Abstract

This paper is an exegesis of 1 Timothy 2:8–15. The passage deals with the behavior and role of men and women in corporate worship, in the context of teaching in the church, and, to a broader degree, in relation to ecclesiastical structure and authority in the early church. Paul encourages men to pray everywhere by lifting holy hands without a spirit of anger or discord. Paul encourages women to dress modestly and to have a spirit of quietness. Also, there is the much-discussed passage where Paul says, "I do not permit a woman to teach or to exercise authority over a man." Paul states that his reasoning for this prohibition comes from the account of the order of creation and the story of the fall in Genesis. We will also consider what Paul meant when he stated that women will be saved through childbearing.

Note on the Exegetical Approach

The exegesis of this passage follows the guidelines of the historical-critical method, meaning the authors will explore matters of grammar (both lexicological and syntactical) and the historical-political-social-cultural background of the passage. Also, both the immediate and remote contexts of the passage will be considered. Finally, the passage will be viewed through a Christocentric lens. The goal is to discover what Paul meant when he wrote these words to Timothy almost two thousand years ago. (The authors of this paper believe that Paul was the author of 1 Timothy, and Paul was writing to his young protege Timothy who was located in Ephesus at the time.)

The Conduct of Men and Women. 2:8–15

UBS[48]

⁸Βούλομαι οὖν προσεύχεσθαι τοὺς ἄνδρας ἐν παντὶ τόπῳ ἐπαίροντας ὁσίους χεῖρας χωρὶς ὀργῆς καὶ διαλογισμοῦ. ⁹ὡσαύτως [καὶ] γυναῖκας ἐν καταστολῇ κοσμίῳ μετὰ αἰδοῦς καὶ σωφροσύνης κοσμεῖν ἑαυτάς, μὴ ἐν πλέγμασιν καὶ χρυσίῳ ἢ μαργαρίταις ἢ ἱματισμῷ πολυτελεῖ, ¹⁰ἀλλ' ὃ πρέπει γυναιξὶν ἐπαγγελλομέναις θεοσέβειαν, δι' ἔργων ἀγαθῶν. ¹¹γυνὴ ἐν ἡσυχίᾳ μανθανέτω ἐν πάσῃ ὑποταγῇ· ¹²διδάσκειν δὲ γυναικὶ οὐκ ἐπιτρέπω οὐδὲ αὐθεντεῖν ἀνδρός, ἀλλ' εἶναι ἐν ἡσυχίᾳ. ¹³Ἀδὰμ γὰρ πρῶτος ἐπλάσθη, εἶτα Εὕα. ¹⁴καὶ Ἀδὰμ οὐκ ἠπατήθη, ἡ δὲ γυνὴ ἐξαπατηθεῖσα ἐν παραβάσει γέγονεν· ¹⁵σωθήσεται δὲ διὰ τῆς τεκνογονίας, ἐὰν μείνωσιν ἐν πίστει καὶ ἀγάπῃ καὶ ἁγιασμῷ μετὰ σωφροσύνης·

Kinnard's Translation[49]

⁸*Therefore, I wish that men should pray in every place, holding up holy hands without anger and argument.*

⁹*Likewise, women should adorn themselves in appropriate clothing with modesty and moderation, not with braided hair, gold ornaments, pearls or expensive clothing,* ¹⁰*but what is fitting for women who profess godliness through good works.*

¹¹*A woman must learn in quietness, in all submission.* ¹²*I do not permit a woman to teach, neither to exercise authority[50] over a man, but to remain in quietness.* ¹³*For Adam was formed first, then Eve.* ¹⁴*Adam was not deceived, but the woman was deceived and became a transgressor.* ¹⁵*But she will be saved through childbearing, if they remain in faith, love, and holiness with self-control.*

NIV1984[51]

⁸*I want men everywhere to lift up holy hands in prayer, without anger or disputing.*

48. Kurt Aland et al., *The Greek New Testament,* Fourth Revised Edition (with Morphology) (Deutsche Bibelgesellschaft, 1993; 2006), 1 Ti 1:1–2.

49. From the *King Jesus New Testament,* a translation by Dr. G. Steve Kinnard.

50. The word αὐθεντεῖν, *authentein* could also be translated as "usurp authority."

51. *The Holy Bible: New International Version* (Grand Rapids, MI: Zondervan, 1984), Galatians 4:19. Hereafter, NIV1984.

⁹I also want women to dress modestly, with decency and propriety, not with braided hair or gold or pearls or expensive clothes, ¹⁰but with good deeds, appropriate for women who profess to worship God.

¹¹A woman should learn in quietness and full submission. ¹²I do not permit a woman to teach or to have authority over a man; she must be silent. ¹³For Adam was formed first, then Eve. ¹⁴And Adam was not the one deceived; it was the woman who was deceived and became a sinner. ¹⁵But women will be saved through childbearing—if they continue in faith, love and holiness with propriety.

Introduction

As authors we would like to know, when you opened this book, did you skip through the pages to find this particular passage to see what we as teachers had to say about these verses? If you did, we can't blame you. This is one of those controversial passages that demand our attention. In fact, Knute Larson writes about this passage, noting,

This chapter also contains one of the most controversial verses in the Bible, about the place of women in the church. There are many ways to understand this. Ask for wisdom as you study the chapter and for grace toward others who may disagree with the conclusion that becomes your conviction![52]

That's good advice. This is a difficult passage. We should study to understand it, but we should be careful about being too dogmatic. Humility should be our guide in our study and our discussion of these verses.

What is the historical setting here? The setting is the public assembly of the church in Ephesus. The setting includes times where the teaching of Scripture and doctrine occurred in the local assembly of the church. And, when you consider that the passage continues directly into the appointing of elders in chapter four, the broader context is the consideration of the ecclesiastical structure in the church. When the church assembled together in Ephesus, something was out of step. Paul addresses that concern here.

First, we will consider background material. Second, we will look at what Paul has to say to Timothy concerning the men of the church in

52. Knute Larson, *I & II Thessalonians, I & II Timothy, Titus, Philemon,* vol. 9, Holman New Testament Commentary (Nashville, TN: Broadman & Holman Publishers, 2000), 163.

Ephesus. Third, we will explore Paul's comments to Timothy concerning the women in the church there.

Timothy in Ephesus

The Historical, Cultural, Sociological, Archeological, and Geopolitical Background

Ephesus was a huge, cosmopolitan city located in Asia Minor (modern Turkey). It was home to one of the wonders of the ancient world, the Temple of Artemis/Diana. Female priests officiated at this temple. Also, Ephesus had a wonderful library, so people would come to the city to worship and to study.

Some of us have had the opportunity to visit the archaeological ruins of Ephesus. There is a section in Ephesus where the wealthy patrons lived. You can see the ancient frescoes that decorated their homes. They were very elaborate and ornate. Tour guides of the ancient city point out painted footprints that line the city pavement. These painted footprints led to the brothels and houses of prostitution. Guides also point out the public baths that the Romans made popular in Ephesus.

Rome had a major influence on Ephesus. Rome controlled the city. One of the major influences that Rome had on the city was the introduction of the concept of the "new Roman woman" into the society there. Recently, biblical scholars have posited the theory that Paul's writing in 1 Timothy 2 reflects the emergence of the new Roman woman in the eastern part of the empire.[53] Philip H. Towner defines and describes characteristics of this woman, writing,

> She exercised freedoms and opportunities for participation in public life (political and legal activity, patron and benefactor roles) that far exceeded those of the traditional Greek woman, who has long been the model drawn on by NT scholars. Moreover, the ancient evaluation of her patterns of dress and behavior locate her within something of an ancient "sexual revolution."[54]

53. The best source on this topic is Bruce W. Winter's *Roman Wives, Roman Widows: The Appearance of New Women and the Pauline Communities* (Grand Rapids, MI: Eerdmans, 2003).

54. Philip H. Towner, *The Letters to Timothy and Titus.* New International Commentary on the New Testament (Grand Rapids: Eerdmans, 2006), p. 196.

For those of us who lived through the 60s in the United States, we understand the concept of a sexual revolution with all the uninhibited freedoms that went along with this revolution. Ephesus was experiencing the same type of revolution in the 60s. But we are speaking about the 60s of the first century.

The rulers of Rome were not happy with the changes that they saw occurring around the city. Winter writes, "Augustus and some of his successors used appearance and apparel to promote values to counter what they regarded as promiscuous tendencies in the Empire."[55] The introduction of permissive clothing and hairstyles explains why Paul specifically wrote against "braided hair, gold ornaments, pearls, or expensive clothing." This was the style of the new Roman woman. The style lacked modesty. And modesty was to be a characteristic of the Christian woman. Thus Paul directs Timothy to instruct the women in the church to dress modestly. This outward adorning of the body reflects the inner adorning of the heart.

This new fashion style was one way for the new Roman woman to push against repressive boundaries. In general, the men of Rome had much more freedom than the women of Rome. Only men held public office. Ancient Athens and Rome developed the modern democratic society, but only men participated in this democratic society. Men attended the Roman baths; women didn't. Women did not have the same freedoms or opportunities as men. What was the philosophy behind the mindset of the new Roman woman? Towner writes,

> Equally characteristic was the desire of influential women to acquire for themselves and enjoy the freedoms, normally restricted to men, to explore multiple sexual liaisons in association with dinner parties and banquets. Pursuit of sexual freedom required remaining unencumbered with children, so the ancient discussion includes reference to the practices of contraception and abortion. What might appear less drastic were the desires of women to take active roles in public life, in legal contexts sometimes functioning as advocates; but in some cases this simply took the form of speaking up in the presence of men/husbands, offering opinions, teaching, and philosophizing... what has been termed the movement of the "new Roman woman."[56]

---

55. Winter, Kindle Locations 197–198.
56. Towner, p. 48.

Women began to push the boundaries of what was considered respectable behavior of a wife and mother by the elite of Roman society.

This sociological change began in Rome and then headed east. Soon the fashion, styles, and thinking of the new Roman woman invaded Corinth and Ephesus. Towner writes,

> In urban contexts such as Corinth and Ephesus, where wealthy women were numbered among church members, the new movement had apparently made inroads. Matters of dress and behavior of women in Pauline churches were therefore quite likely to have been influenced by the model of the new liberal woman. If the background proves sustainable, then we find Paul reacting to the trends in Corinth that threatened to link the gospel message with a rejection of all the old rules of modesty. This would effectively associate Christianity with immorality in a way that would thoroughly discredit the gospel.[57]

In reading chapter 2, we need to keep in mind this backdrop of the influence of the new Roman woman on society in the Eastern Roman Empire.

The biggest question in 1 Timothy 2 (and one of the biggest questions of hermeneutics) is "What is cultural and what transcends culture?" In verse 9 the idea that transcends culture is Paul's admonition that "women should adorn themselves in appropriate clothing with modesty and moderation." This is the primary point that Paul is making in these verses. In Ephesus, immodest apparel would include braided hair, gold ornaments, pearls, or expensive clothing. However, those are cultural items. Notice he doesn't mention a veil/covering. He does in 1 Corinthians 11. Why the difference? Perhaps this is because the cultural norms of Ephesus and Corinth were different. Expressions of modesty are different in different cultures. What transcends culture is for women (and men) to dress modestly and live modest lives within their culture. How that is achieved changes from culture to culture.

In his list, Paul begins with braided hair. Towner writes, "The term that means literally 'braiding' refers to the complex and fancy styling of hair—plaiting and piling it on top of the head—preferred by fashionable women of a certain sort."[58] This type of braiding was expensive. It was often accompanied by gold beads and pearls being braided into elaborate hairstyles.

57. Towner, p. 48.
58. Towner, p. 208.

Next, Paul mentions "gold ornaments" and "pearls." Winter notes, "Pearls could be another epitome for sumptuousness."[59] Jewelry became "emblematic of the shameful woman."[60]

Paul concludes his list by mentioning expensive clothes. Elaborate hairstyles, lavish jewelry, and expensive clothes were the hallmarks of the new Roman woman.

The hallmark of the new Christian woman/wife was different. Instead of being adorned with expensive clothes, the new Christian woman was to adorn herself in good works. Good works/good deeds were considered the fruit of a godly life.

In every culture Christian men and women must understand what is culturally appropriate and inappropriate, then they must act and dress accordingly. Consider 1 Peter 3:3–4. Peter addresses Christian wives in this passage. He writes, "Your beauty should not come from outward adornment, such as braided hair and the wearing of gold jewelry and fine clothes. Instead, it should be that of your inner self, the unfading beauty of a gentle and quiet spirit, which is of great worth in God's sight." Peter is associated with Antioch. That is farther east than Ephesus. His main idea was that true beauty lies inside a person, in a gentle and quiet spirit. This idea transcends culture. However, he does mention three specific cultural items—braided hair, gold jewelry, and fine clothes. This list differs slightly from Paul's list in 1 Timothy 2. Paul includes pearls in his list. The fact that the two lists do not match exactly may demonstrate that the lists are cultural, not universal (transcultural). The universal idea expressed in both lists is that Christians should study their culture, determine what is modest and immodest, and act accordingly. Lea and Griffen write, "Although Paul discussed dress, his true emphasis was not merely that women should dress modestly but that genuine ornamentation is not external at all and consists of an attitude of commitment to good works."[61] In every culture, disciples of Jesus are to dress in a way that allows the inner beauty of their heart to demonstrate to the world that they love God and live their lives for his glory.

---

59. Winter, Kindle Locations 1265–1266.
60. Towner, p. 208.
61. Thomas D. Lea and Hayne P. Griffin, *1, 2 Timothy, Titus,* vol. 34, The New American Commentary (Nashville: Broadman & Holman Publishers, 1992), 96.

Paul Addresses the Men

V. 8. *Therefore, I wish that men should pray in every place, holding up holy hands without anger and argument.*

Paul addresses the men and then the women concerning worship. He has something to say to each group.

To the men, Paul says that he wishes that the men would pray in every place. "Wish" carries with it an implication of expectation (Βούλομαι, *boulomai*). An alternate translation would be, "I desire."

"In every place" could mean "every place of worship," and it is translated as such in the *New Living Translation*. "Every place" could refer to various house churches that met in Ephesus. Also, Paul could be expressing a broader idea here. He desires for men to pray everywhere. Whichever way it is taken, prayer is closely associated with worship.

When men pray, they should hold up holy hands without an angry or contentious spirit. There appears to have been some type of strife occurring in the church in Ephesus. Whatever the problem was, Paul did not want the problem to enter the context of public worship. Instead, anger and arguments were to cease before corporate worship began.

This passage reminds us of the words of Jesus in the Sermon on the Mount, "Therefore, if you are offering your gift at the altar and there remember that your brother or sister has something against you, leave your gift there in front of the altar. First go and be reconciled to them; then come and offer your gift" (Matthew 5:23–24). Before we worship, we must check our attitude toward other people. If we need to be reconciled with another disciple before worship begins, then reconciliation precedes worship.

Getting rid of this type of animosity would be symbolized by "holy hands." "Holding up holy hands" also implies a purity for worship. This again underscores the fact that in 1 Timothy 2 the context is the corporate worship of the church.

In this passage, we have to ask, "What is cultural and what transcends culture?" Prayer transcends culture. It is universal. It can occur at any location and at any time. Worshipping God without anger transcends culture. We are to worship God and pray to God with the right attitude.

However, "holy hands" could be cultural. How do we know that? The fact that this term is not understood in all cultures could indicate that it is cultural. Plus, not everyone can hold up "holy hands." Some people don't have the use of their arms. Consider this: In Greek culture, it is an insult to show someone the palm of your hand. In that culture, you ought to think twice before you lift your hand to God.

In first-century Jewish culture, devout Jews washed their hands before prayer. They dried their hands by lifting them in the air and letting them drip dry. (This still occurs in certain sects of Judaism). This was a way of showing God that they approached him with clean hands.

Today, we can lift holy hands in prayer, but we can also lift up our hands in our hearts by having a pure heart when we approach God. The physical washing of the hands isn't as important as the spiritual washing of the heart. God wants us to approach him with a pure heart.

Mounce summarizes this verse in his commentary on the Pastoral Epistles, writing, "The imagery of ὁσίους χεῖρας, "holy hands," comes from the OT (Exodus 30:19–21; Ps 24:4; Isa 1:15, 59:3), which requires that hands be ritually clean before approaching God; the cleansing later became moral (cf. Jas 4:8; 1 Pet 3:7). Jesus himself insisted that 'reconciliation must precede worship' (Stott, 82; cf. Matt 5:23–24, 6:12, 14–15; Mark 11:25). The topic of prayer does not arise again in this passage, showing that prayer is not the main concern." So what is the main concern?[62] That is a literary device known as foreshadowing. Foreshadowing keeps the reader reading. Paul introduces other ideas concerning propriety and attitude in the assembly of disciples and public worship. So, let's keep reading.

Paul Addresses the Women

> **Vv. 9–10.** *⁹Likewise, women should adorn themselves in appropriate clothing with modesty and moderation, not with braided hair, gold ornaments, pearls or expensive clothing, ¹⁰but what is fitting for women who profess godliness through good works.*

---

62. William D. Mounce, *Pastoral Epistles,* vol. 46, Word Biblical Commentary (Dallas: Word, Incorporated, 2000), 108.

(Look at the section above entitled "The Historical, Cultural, Sociological, Archeological, and Geopolitical Background" for information on these verses.)

Vv. 11–15. *[11]A woman must learn in quietness, in all submission. [12]I do not permit a woman to teach, neither to exercise authority over a man, but to remain in quietness. [13]For Adam was formed first, then Eve. [14]Adam was not deceived, but the woman was deceived and became a transgressor. [15]But she will be saved through childbearing, if they remain in faith, love and holiness with self-control.*

This is an important passage. It is also a difficult one. It is the passage used most often to teach that women should not be in a position of ecclesiastical authority over men. Therefore, it is a highly controversial scripture.

We need to answer some questions as we look at this passage. First, what was Paul saying to his original readers? How did Timothy understand the passage? Second, what part of the passage is cultural and should remain in its first-century context, and what transcends culture and should be applied today?

So, let's explore this passage in order to understand what it says and what it doesn't say.

V. 11. *A woman must learn in quietness, in all submission.*

Again, the context is the assembly of the church. In the assembly of believers, Paul wants the church environment to be conducive to learning. It seems there was a problem with this in Ephesus (and in Corinth). Therefore, Paul writes to young Timothy in order to instruct him in regard to how to make the environment of the assembly more conducive to learning.

Paul wants women to be able to learn in the assembly. This stands in contrast to the Jewish temple setting in Jerusalem, where women were only allowed in the women's court (the outer court) and not in the inner court with the men. Many believe that this separation of the genders was also true in synagogue worship. It is still true in the Hasidic Jewish community and in other communities around the world. However, in the early church, men and women were together in worship, participating and sharing together. At least that seems to be the case. Some scholars believe that the church in Corinth was segregated, and that men worshipped in one room and women in another room. This occurred because of the influence of Jewish Christians in that setting. However, most scholars believe that in Ephesus, the men and women assembled together. In that setting, women were to learn in quietness and submission.

To learn in quietness and submission doesn't mean women must never talk or never say anything in the assembly. Some translations translate "quietness" (ἡσυχίᾳ, *hēsychia*) as "silence," but "quietness" is a better translation. Paul isn't looking for an external response. Paul seeks for an internal, intrinsic quality to manifest itself. Thus "quietness" is a better translation here. In this context, quietness connects with submission and points to an intrinsic definition of ἡσυχίᾳ (*hēsychia*). Quietness and submission are a matter of the heart.

Paul wanted to make sure that the conditions of the assembly were conducive to learning so the women would have an opportunity to learn. He is especially concerned that the women were able to learn. This was a progressive thought in Paul's day.

Paul says let the women learn in quietness and submission. This is the way men should learn as well. Anyone who is teachable should have a quiet and submissive heart. This allows the heart to be teachable.

V. 12. *Paul moves to the next topic. He writes, I do not permit a woman to teach, neither to exercise authority over a man, but to remain in quietness.*

Volumes have been written about this verse.[63] Paul states that women are not to teach men or to exercise authority over men. This applies directly to the assembly of the church, although given the broader context of the passage and how this passage leads into chapter 3 and the discussion of selecting elders, Paul could also have an ecclesiastical structure in mind.

Perhaps Paul is continuing his earlier thought in verses 9–10 where he has the "new Roman woman" in mind. The new Roman woman was

---

63. See *Discovering Biblical Equality,* gen. eds. Ronald W. Pierce and Rebecca Merrill Groothuis (Downers Grove: IVP Academic), 2005 and *Recovering Biblical Manhood and Womanhood* (Wheaton: Crossway Books).

pushing the boundaries of the woman's role in society in an ungodly manner. Paul warns against the influence of this new Roman woman in the church. Paul Larson writes,

> It could be that as women experienced new freedoms within the Christian community, they began to throw off restraint. Their disagreements, questions, and assertions then became not a learning experience but a disruption that worked against true worship. Paul did not want the women to be contentious. His main concern was the establishment of orderly worship.[64]

So Paul instructs Timothy that women are neither to teach nor to exercise authority over men.

A big question is what did Paul mean by "exercise authority?" The term "exercise authority" is extremely difficult to translate because the Greek word, αὐθεντέω (*authenteō*) is a *hapax legomenon,* meaning it is used only once in the NT. Some scholars say the term carries with it a negative, even a hostile, connotation of "do not usurp authority," "do not seize control." Thus, women can have authority over men in an ecclesiastical setting as long as they don't "seize" control. Other scholars view the term in a more general sense as, "do not have authority over." If the word is viewed in this way, then women are not allowed to have authority over men in any ecclesiastical setting. Scholarship is extremely divided over this issue, and there seems to be no way to reconcile the two camps.[65] So, we need to look at other passages for help here.

The same dynamic that we see in Ephesus must have existed in Corinth. When Paul writes about the assembly of believers in Corinth in 1 Corinthians 14:33b–35, he states,

> As in all the congregations of the saints, [34]women should remain silent in the churches. They are not allowed to speak, but must be in submission, as the Law says. [35]If they want to inquire about something, they should ask their own husbands at home; for it is disgraceful for a woman to speak in the church.[66]

64. Larson, p. 169.
65. Compare *Discovering Biblical Equality,* gen. eds. Ronald W. Pierce and Rebecca Merrill Groothuis (Downers Grove: IVP Academic), 2005 and *Recovering Biblical Manhood and Womanhood* (Wheaton: Crossway Books) and Cynthia Long Westfall, Paul and Gender (Grand Rapids: Baker Academic).
66. *The Holy Bible: New International Version* (Grand Rapids, MI: Zondervan, 1984), 1 Co 14:33–35.

We know that in Corinth women prayed and prophesied in the assembly (1 Corinthians 11). Therefore, Paul is not talking about absolute silence. Women are allowed to participate in corporate worship. Perhaps Paul was prohibiting the "taking over" or the "control" of the worship of the church.

In Paul's letter to Timothy, we learn that Paul did not permit the women to teach in the setting of corporate worship. However, this did not mean that women could not teach in the church. Women could be teachers, as older women were instructed to teach other women (Titus 2:3–5) as well as children (2 Timothy 1:5), and in a team effort, Priscilla and Aquila taught Apollos (Acts 18:25–26). Anna was a prophetess (Luke 2:36–38), and Philip's daughters prophesied (Acts 21:9). However, Paul was clear to Timothy that women were not to teach men or to exercise authority in the ecclesiastical context.

What type of teaching is Paul talking about here? It must be something other than praying and prophesying, because he allowed women to pray and prophesy in the church in Corinth (1 Corinthians 14). Teaching here seems to be a more authorized and ecclesiastical type of teaching within the church. Throughout the letter, teaching is paired with "command and teach" and "urge and teach." Also, the letter is filled with matters of doctrine and doctrinal concerns. Lea and Griffin propose,

> Teaching involved official doctrinal instruction in the Scriptures (1 Tim 5:17) and was a task delegated to the pastor-teacher (Eph 4:11). The heavy emphasis in the Pastorals on proper doctrine (1 Tim 1:10; 4:6, 13, 16; 6:1, 3; *didaskalia*) implies the need for a trusted source of doctrine.[67]

Understanding Paul's instruction to Timothy regarding women, we go to the question that must be asked for us today: What instructions here were specifically cultural, and what part of these instructions transcends culture? Clearly, those women in Timothy's ministry were not permitted to hold ecclesiastical authority. Is that an instruction for us today? Could this be because women were not taught? We do not know the answers to these questions. Just as we view the prohibition of jewelry as a cultural phenomenon, understanding the circumstances of Paul's

---

67. Lea and Griffen, p. 99.

particular audience, can we likewise recognize the prohibition of women teaching men in a cultural sense? Or, do we see that as a command for all time?

Clearly, Paul's intention was not to exclude women from using their gifts and abilities in the context of the corporate church meeting. However, the "universal principles" that we can apply have to do with decorum and demeanor. No woman, or man for that matter, should take it upon himself or herself to usurp authority or have a domineering manner. And it seems that in the setting that Paul is addressing, the women were more likely to be guilty of this act. Twenty-first-century readers of the Scriptures can learn from these passages and apply them in our present-day situations.

In our interpretation, Paul teaches that men and women have different offices in the ministry. Both men and women can use their God-given gifts of leadership, encouragement, prophecy, teaching, and serving in the ministry.

How then, do we interpret Paul's exhortation about the women as it segues into his example that goes back to creation?

Vv. 13–14. *[13]For Adam was formed first, then Eve. [14]Adam was not deceived, but the woman was deceived and became a transgressor.*

The word γάρ (*gar*) is used in this context to express "cause" or "reason."[68] For this context, it is more likely that Paul is stating the "reason" for his prohibition, not the cause. Paul now gives the reason for his previous comments.

Paul undergirds his teaching by reaching all the way back to the created order of things. George W. Knight notes, "The ground for the prohibition is now given: It is the order of the creation of Adam and Eve as the archetypes of man and woman and the implication of this order for headship and submission in such relationships."[69] Other scholars

68. William Arndt, Frederick W. Danker, and Walter Bauer, *A Greek-English Lexicon of the New Testament and Other Early Christian Literature* (Chicago: University of Chicago Press, 2000), 189.

68. George W. Knight, *The Pastoral Epistles: A Commentary of the Greek Text,* New International Greek Testament Commentary (Grand Rapids, MI; Carlisle, England: W.B. Eerdmans; Paternoster Press, 1992), 142.

note Paul's rabbinical training and the heresies promoted in Ephesus to explain his reasoning.[70]

Paul is not saying that Adam (man) was not guilty of transgression in the fall. He states Adam's guilt in Romans 5:12ff. His sin was more egregious since he sinned with his eyes wide open. However, Paul is citing these references in Genesis to give the reason behind what he is saying to Timothy in this epistle. Notice that Paul does not just reference the fall in his argument, but he also references the created order before the fall.

V. 15. *But she will be saved through childbearing, if they remain in faith, love and holiness with self-control.*

There are several ways to understand this verse.

First, taken literally, when a woman bears a child, the act of childbearing saves her. There are at least two reasons to reject this interpretation: (1) It is inconsistent with other scriptures that teach that we are not saved by works. (2) It is not possible for some women to have children. Since God wants all people to be saved, he cannot be saying that for a woman to be saved she must bear a child.

Second, in the Greco-Roman world of the first century, when women gave birth, there was a high risk that the mother would die in the

---

70. Within the synagogue, which provided a model for early church life and structure, male dominance in Jewish culture was traditionally validated by the chronological sequence of creation in Genesis 2. Men were created first, therefore they were in charge (in 1 Cor 11:8–9 Paul uses the chronological sequence of Genesis 2 to build his teaching that women wear head coverings.) In 2 Cor. 11:3–4 Paul uses Eve's deception to illustrate that all believers in Corinth may be deceived and led from faith in Christ. Paul uses the Eve tradition in different ways, depending on the problem he is addressing. In both Ephesus and Corinth, it is a possibility that false teaching is at the heart of his concerns. The discussions of who was created first and who sinned first could be related to the false teachings, particularly in Ephesus where false teachers were misleading people to follow Satan (1 Tim 2:8), tempting the women to adorn themselves provocatively, stirring up anger with the men, and raising up female teachers to dominate the men to promote the heresy, particularly in light of the teachings of Artemis. Sarah Sumner, *Men and Women in the Church* (Downers Grove: InterVarsity Press, 2003), 259–261; Bruce K. Waltke, editor D.A. Carson, *The Enduring Authority of the Christian Scriptures* (Grand Rapids: Eerdmans, 2016), 570, and F.F. Bruce, Manfred Brauch, Peter Davids, and Walter Kaiser Jr., *Hard Sayings of the Bible* (Downers Grove: InterVarsity, 1996), 669–670.

process of childbirth. Women were often married at fourteen or fifteen, and they became pregnant immediately after their marriage. Their bodies were not ready to have a child. So, to salve their fears of dying during childbirth, the women of Ephesus would sometimes turn to the Temple of Artemis for comfort and assurance. Paul connects safety in bearing children with remaining faithful to Jesus. He is exhorting the female disciples in Ephesus not to turn to Artemis, but to turn to Jesus, or better, to stick with Jesus. Paul says, "remain in faith, love and holiness with self-control."

Third, consider the whole passage and consider the wider context. One of the differences between men and women is that women can have children and men can't. Paul is possibly speaking of women being willing to accept their role of being wives and mothers, and they should accept their role with quietness and submission. This is a matter of the heart. It is an inner attitude. Thus it becomes a matter of salvation. Women are to accept their role and remain in faith, love, and holiness with self-control.

Fourth, we take this verse as referring to the bearing of the child— Jesus. The verse refers to Mary's humble act of submission and the fact that Jesus came into the world because she submitted to God's will. Taken this way, salvation comes into the world through the act of *"the* Childbearing," the act of Jesus coming into the world.

Paul goes on and describes the leadership roles in the church more specifically in the next chapter. In the original text, there would be no chapter markers. This passage would flow right into the passage on elders (the ecclesiastical hierarchy and authority of the early church). In this section of the letter, Paul writes about leadership roles within the church, and he is answering a problem that arose in the worship and teaching ministry in Ephesus.

Bibliography

Kurt Aland et al., *The Greek New Testament,* Fourth Revised Edition (with Morphology). Deutsche Bibelgesellschaft, 1993; 2006.

Bailey, Kenneth E. *Jesus Through Middle Eastern Eyes.* Downers Grove, IL: IVP Academic, 2007.

Bauer, W. A *Greek-English Lexicon of the New Testament and Other Early Christian Literature,* trs. W. F. Arndt and F. W. Gingrich, 2nd Ed. Rev. and augmented by F. W. Gingrich and F. W. Danker from Bauer's 5th ed, (1958), Chicago, 1979.

Bauckham, Richard. *Gospel Women: Studies of the Named Women in the Gospels.* Grand Rapids: Eerdmans, 2015.

Belleville, Linda L. *Women Leaders and the Church: Three Crucial Questions.* Ada, MI: Revell, 2000.

Belleville, Linda L., Craig L. Blomberg, Craig S. Keener, and Thomas R. Schreiner. *Two Views on Women in Ministry.* Grand Rapids: Zondervan, 2009.

Cohick, Lynn. *Women in the World of the Earliest Christians: Illuminating Ancient Ways of Life.* Grand Rapids, MI: Baker, 2009.

Curtis James, Carolyn. *Malestrom: Manhood Swept into the Currents of a Changing World.* Grand Rapids: Zondervan, 2015.

Discovering Biblical Equality, gen. eds. Ronald W. Pierce and Rebecca Merrill Groothuis, Downers Grove: IVP Academic, 2005.

Fee, Gordon D. 1 *and 2 Timothy, Titus.* New International Biblical Commentary. Peabody, MA: Hendrickson Publishers, Inc., 1995.

Ferguson, Everett. *Women in the Church.* Chickasha, OK: Yeoman Press, 2003.

Guthrie, Donald. *The Pastoral Epistles.* Tyndale New Testament Commentaries. Downers Grove: InterVarsity Press, 1990.

Hendricksen, William and Simon j. Kistemaker. Thessalonians, *The Pastorals and Hebrews.* Nashville: Baker Books, 1996.

Highfield, Ron. *Four Views on Women and Church Leadership.* Los Angeles: Keledei Publications, 2017.

The IVP Women's Bible Commentary, Eds. Catherine Clark Kroeger and Mary J. Evans, Downers Grove: InterVarsity Press, 2002.

Kelly, J. N. D. *The Pastoral Epistles,* Black's New Testament Commentary. London: Continuum, 1963.

Kenner, Craig S. *Paul, Women, and Wives: Marriage and Women's Ministry in the Letters of Paul.* Grand Rapids: Baker Academic, 2004.

Knight, George W. III, *Commentary of the Pastoral Epistles.* New International Greek Testament Commentary. Grand Rapids, MI: William B. Eerdmans Publishing Company, 1992.

Larson, Knute. *I & II Thessalonians, I & II Timothy, Titus, Philemon,* vol. 9. Holman New Testament Commentary. Nashville, TN: Broadman & Holman Publishers, 2000.

Lea, T. D., and Griffin, H. P. *1, 2 Timothy, Titus.* Volume 34. The New American Commentary. Nashville: Holman Reference, 1992.

Lee-Barnewall, Michelle. *Neither Complementarian nor Egalitarian: A Kingdom Corrective to the Evangelical Gender Debate.* Grand Rapids: Baker Academic, 2016.

Louw, Johannes P. and Eugene Albert Nida, *Greek-English Lexicon of the New Testament: Based on Semantic Domains.* New York: United Bible Societies, 1996.

Marshall, I. Howard. *The Pastoral Epistles.* The International Critical Commentary. London, UK: T&T Clark, 1999.

Mounce, William D. *Pastoral Epistles,* vol. 46, Word Biblical Commentary. Dallas: Word, Incorporated, 2000.

McKnight, Scot. *The Blue Parakeet: Rethinking How You Read the Bible.* Grand Rapids: Zondervan. 2008.

_____. *Junia Is Not Alone: Breaking Our Silence About Women in the Bible and the Church Today.* Englewood, Co: Patheos, 2011.

Osburn, Carroll. Women in the Church. Abilene, TX: ACU Press, 2001.

Pierce, R. W., Groothuis, R. M., and Fee, G. D. (2005). *Discovering Biblical Equality: Complementarity Without Hierarchy.* Downers Grove, IL: InterVarsity Press.

Recovering Biblical Manhood and Womanhood, Editors John Piper and Wayne Grudem Wheaton: Crossway Books.

Sumner, Sarah. *Men and Women in the Church.* Downers Grove: InterVarsity Press, 2003.

Thomas R. Schreiner, *Interpreting the Pauline Epistles,* Second Edition. Grand Rapids, MI: Baker Academic, 2011.

Thomas C. Oden, *First and Second Timothy and Titus,* Interpretation. Louisville: John Knox Press, 1989.

Towner, Philip H. *The Letters to Timothy and Titus.* New International Commentary on the New Testament. Grand Rapids: Eerdmans, 2006.

Webb, William. Slaves, *Women and Homosexuals: Exploring the Hermeneutics of Cultural Analysis.* Downers Grove, IL: InterVarsity Press, 2001.

Westfall, Cynthia Long. *Paul and Gender: Reclaiming the Apostle's Vision for Men and Women in Christ.* Grand Rapids, MI: Baker Academic, 2016.

Winter, Bruce W. *Roman Wives, Roman Widows: The Appearance of New Women and the Pauline Communities.* Grand Rapids, MI: Eerdmans, 2003.

Witherington III, Ben. *Women in the Earliest Churches.* Cambridge: Cambridge University Press, 1988.

_____. *Women in the Ministry of Jesus.* Cambridge: Cambridge University Press, 1984.

Women's Bible Commentary, Edited by Carol A. Newsom and Sharon H. Ringe; 2nd ed. Louisville: Westminster John Knox, 1998.

Women in Scripture. Edited by Carol Meyers. Boston: Houghton Mifflin Company, 2000.

Wright, NT. *Paul for Everyone: The Pastoral Letters: 1 and 2 Timothy and Titus.* London: Society for Promoting Christian Knowledge, 2004.

Zehr, Paul M. *1 & 2 Timothy, Titus,* Believers Church Bible Commentary. Scottdale, PA; Waterloo, ON: Herald Press, 2010.

Yarbrough, Robert W. *The Letters to Timothy and Titus.* The Pillar New Testament Commentary. Grand Rapids, MI: Eerdmans, 2018.

CHAPTER SEVEN

Titus 2:3–5

Suzette Lewis
Dr. Scott Warlow

Abstract

In Titus 2:3–5, Paul is instructing Titus to teach the older women in the church in Crete regarding their role in helping the younger women to mature in love and holiness. This paper considers the historical and cultural background in first-century Crete and the Roman Empire more broadly and whether the behavior Paul expects from the older and younger women is purely culturally based, or in some ways transcends culture.

The NIV text of Titus 2:3–5 reads as follows:

> ³*Likewise, teach the older women to be reverent in the way they live, not to be slanderers or addicted to much wine, but to teach what is good.* ⁴*Then they can urge the younger women to love their husbands and children,* ⁵*to be self-controlled and pure, to be busy at home, to be kind, and to be subject to their husbands, so that no one will malign the word of God.*

Historical and Cultural Context

To interpret the passage properly, it is important to gain a full understanding of the historical and cultural context of the passage, both on the island of Crete and more broadly in the Roman Empire, as well as the overall picture of what was happening in the churches in Crete that prompted Paul to write the letter to Titus.

Crete is referred to in Acts 27 (verses 7, 12, 13 and 21), as well as Acts 2:11 (i.e., some of those converted on the Day of Pentecost were likely from Crete). The island is located in the Mediterranean Sea, south of Greece and Asia Minor. It fell to Rome and was made a Roman province in 71 BC. Its legal code provided women with freedoms and rights not enjoyed by women in the rest of the Greek and Roman world. Its people were known for claiming that Zeus was born and died on

Crete, and this led to the common perception that Cretans are liars (see Titus 1:12–13). Crete also had a reputation for its people being self-indulgent, belligerent, wild, and immoral. It was not unusual for Jewish teachers to be influenced by pagan culture and become forceful teachers of secular values. Paul seems to focus on reluctance to pull back from Cretan cultural norms more than on doctrinal error.

Beginning in the mid–first century BC, there was a cultural phenomenon that arose in Roman society that has been referred to by scholars[71] as the "new Roman woman." This refers to married women or widows of high position who nevertheless engaged in a life of sexual indulgence, primarily with younger, single men. They were essentially intent on exercising the same sexual freedom as was accorded to married men of similar social standing. To continue with such a lifestyle, it was important that the new Roman woman not have any children; unintended pregnancies would be aborted. Evidence for the phenomenon of the new Roman woman can be found among writers (such as Cicero, Tacitus, and Plutarch), poets, and playwrights (such as Catullus and Ovid), as well as philosophers (both Stoic and Neo-Pythagorean) of the period, and in legislation of the time under Augustus, who was apparently attempting to halt the phenomenon by actively promoting the traditional role of married women. Specifically, adultery was made a crime applicable to women only, to be tried in public; prior to that, a husband was within his rights to kill a wife caught in adultery. The charge of adultery had to be brought forward by the husband following a formal divorce, and there were penalties for failing to do so. A woman convicted of adultery would lose half her marriage dowry and one-third of her property, and would be relegated to an island; she was required to wear the toga as a symbol of her infidelity, and she could no longer enter into a fully legal marriage. Men in the Senatorial and Equestrian orders were encouraged to marry and have children, and there were penalties for failing to do so.

The phenomenon of the new Roman woman has been interpreted by Bruce Winter and others as revealing that the traditional model of the ideal Roman wife was in jeopardy of being subverted. Because of the influence of Roman cultural values upon other regions of the empire,

71. A useful resource for research in this area and its value in understanding the cultural background of the New Testament is the book, *Roman Wives, Roman Widows: The Appearance of New Women and the Pauline Communities,* by Bruce Winter.

these scholars believe it is reasonable to conclude that the phenomenon of the new Roman woman was also having some impact in other parts of the Roman Empire, particularly the large wealthy cities, such as Ephesus and Corinth, which had significant Roman populations. This does indeed appear to be a plausible assumption, but it must be recognized that direct evidence of the influence of the new Roman woman upon the cultural milieu in Crete is lacking. Indeed, Winter's conclusions with regard to the seriousness of the threat of the new Roman woman to the ideal of the Roman wife have been challenged by Lynn Cohick,[72] who has provided a substantive argument that the new Roman woman was "more a poetic fiction and a political smear than a historical reality." If Cohick is correct, and Winter has misinterpreted the impact of the phenomenon of the new Roman woman on Roman society, then the same would likely apply in Ephesus. The point here is to note that the phenomenon of the new Roman woman may have had an impact on Cretan society, but that is only a possibility based on plausible inference and not a certainty. We shall see that it can help to make sense of some of Paul's instructions to Titus in the context surrounding our passage.

Paul's letter to Titus clearly presumes a church/mission situation in which false teachers/opponents are present. The opposing message is labeled as "Jewish myths" in Titus 1:14, and Titus 3:9 also uses the term "genealogies" to apply to its content. Disputes tied to the false teaching are referred to as "battles over the law" in 3:9, and similar disruption is tied to the opponents' activities in Titus 1:10–11.

Literary and Linguistic Context

Titus 2:3–5 is located within the larger section Titus 2:1–15 (i.e., all of chapter 2), in which Paul exhorts Titus regarding the teaching of the older men (v. 2), the older women (v. 3), the younger women (vv. 4–5), the younger men (vv. 6–8), and slaves (vv. 9–10) to lead lives that make the gospel attractive. Verses 2–10 act as a form of "household code," specifying behavior that is appropriate within God's household—such

---

72. See Lynn Cohick, *Women in the World of the Earliest Christians: Illuminating Ancient Ways of Life* (Grand Rapids, MI: Baker, 2009), 75. Cynthia Long Westfall agrees with Cohick; see Cynthia Long Westfall, *Paul and Gender: Reclaiming the Apostle's Vision for Men and Women in Christ* (Grand Rapids, MI: Baker Academic, 2016), 15.

codes can be found in the New Testament in passages such as Colossians 3:18–4:1 and Ephesians 5:22–6:9, and were common within Roman culture, although the New Testament codes were unusual in specifying obligations of those in positions of authority (i.e., husbands toward wives, fathers toward children, and masters toward slaves).

The section 2:1–15 is prefaced in 2:1 with an imperative that Titus speak what is in accord with sound teaching. In verses 11–14, Paul provides the grounds for verses 2–10 by stating the ultimate purpose of making the gospel attractive, and he concludes in verse 15 with a repetition of the imperative to speak and exhort with all authority.

Exegesis of Titus 2:3–5

Verse 3 begins with "likewise," tying it to the previous instruction in verse 2 that Titus teach the older men to be self-controlled, worthy of respect, etc. Paul's desire is that Titus ensure that the older women have a demeanor worthy of respect, reflecting holiness, not being false accusers or given to much wine. The compound adjective that follows, καλοδιδασκάλους (*kalodidaskalous* – literally "good teachers"), does not appear elsewhere in the New Testament.[73] It is often translated as "able to teach what is good" in English versions, focused more on the content of the teaching than on the quality of the teacher, but as Towner has emphasized,[74] there is nothing inherent in the word that requires this. Since the three previous injunctions deal with qualities of the older women's behavior, and the four appear together in the pattern "A, b-b, A"; "good" likely applies to both the older women as teachers as well as to their instruction.

Paul reveals in verses 4 and 5 why he desires that the older women be taught these things by Titus—specifically, for the purpose of instructing the younger married women to practice personal behavior that is becoming, shows good judgment, and does not lead to the word of God being maligned. The behavior is itemized in three pairs:

1. to be fond of their husbands and children;

---

73. Indeed, part of the difficulty in interpreting Titus 2:3–5 is that there are multiple words that are compound adjectives that do not appear elsewhere in the New Testament.

74. Philip H. Towner, *The Letters to Timothy and Titus*. The New International Commentary on the New Testament (Grand Rapids, MI: Eerdmans, 2006), 724.

2. to be self-controlled and pure;

3. to be good homemakers and subject to their own husbands.

There is uncertainty regarding the pair of adjectives οἰκουργούςἀγαθάς (oikourgousagathas – "homemakers" and "good"), with regard to whether "good" is to modify "homemakers" or is to be considered as a separate character quality. Several English translations, including the NIV, NASB, and NLT, separate "homemakers" and "good" (usually taken as "kind"), whereas the NRSV has "good homemakers." Witherington has the latter,[75] whereas Towner has the former.[76] Perkins' exegetical handbook has the latter,[77] as does Banker's semantic and structural analysis of Titus.[78] If we read it as "good homemakers," then there are three pairs; the outer two pairs deal with behavior in the home, whereas the inner pair deals with behavior more generally. The word translated as "subject" (ὑποτασσομένας – *hupotassomenas*) is a participle in the middle voice, which implies willing submission for their own benefit. The older women are to teach the younger women these things so that the word of God might not be maligned. Note that the behavior that is required of the older women is different from that required of the younger women and is similar to that expected of deacons' wives in 1 Timothy 3:11. The older women are to behave in a way that is worthy of respect. Nevertheless, they must clearly also abide by the behavior expected of the younger women as well.

There is uncertainty[79] regarding what is referred to by the

---

75. Ben Witherington, *A Socio-Rhetorical Commentary on Titus, 1-2 Timothy and 1-3 John, Letters and Homilies for Hellenized Christians*, vol. 1 (Downers Grove, IL: InterVarsity Press, 2006), 128.

76. Towner, Titus, 717. Towner cites the syntax of the passage—that there are no conjunctions joining any of the adjectives in the series—as the reason for separating them.

77. Larry J. Perkins, *The Pastoral Letters: A Handbook on the Greek Text,* Baylor Handbook on the Greek New Testament (Waco, TX: Baylor University Press, 2017), 258.

78. John Banker, *A Semantic and Structural Analysis of Titus* (Dallas TX: Summer Institute of Linguistics, 1987), 67. Banker cites the symmetry of the qualities for older women in verse 3 and the obvious pairing of the first four qualities for the younger women in verses 4–5 as reasons for not separating them.

79. See J. Harold Greenlee, *An Exegetical Summary of Titus & Philemon,* Second ed. (Dallas, TX: Summer Institute of Linguistics, 2008), 54.

conjunction ἵνα (*hina* – "in order that") in verse 5 (that precedes the desired result that the word of God not be maligned):

1. Is it the last pair of qualities in verse 5?
2. Is it the entire list of six qualities in verses 4–5 expected of the young women?
3. Is it all the qualities in verses 3–5 expected of the older and younger women?

The same conjunction occurs in verse 8 regarding the young men and in verse 10 regarding slaves, with the same desired result of making the gospel attractive, but there is no such conjunction regarding the older men in verse 2. Given the expressed intention of the entire section 2:1–15, it would seem that option (3) is most likely and (1) least likely here, but we cannot be definitive.

Verse 5 seems to indicate that Paul's concern was that the women, both older and younger, not bring shame upon the church by acting in a way that was culturally inappropriate—outsiders would assume that the inappropriate behavior was approved of by the church. The household was the fundamental unit of Greco-Roman society, and those under authority (such as wives) were expected to behave in a way that brought honor, not shame, to the head of the household. To do otherwise was considered subversive and contrary to the normal order of life, and would be regarded with suspicion. Paul was attempting to ensure that the older and younger women behaved in a manner that made the gospel attractive and facilitated the growth of the church.

There are (at least) two questions regarding Paul's instructions here to Titus:

1. Was the model of behavior expressed for the young women entirely dependent on the culture in Crete, or were there parts of that model that transcended culture, and if so, which parts?
2. Was Paul being proactive or reactive in his instruction to Titus, i.e., were the younger (or older) women already behaving in a way that brought the word of God into disrepute, or was Paul trying to ensure that it didn't happen?

The problem in the case of (1) is that some aspects of the model of behavior seem cultural, whereas some aspects appear to transcend the surrounding culture. The question is then: is the requirement that the wife be willingly subject to her husband cultural or transcultural? It is clearly consistent with what is considered desirable in the local culture in Crete and is therefore consistent with the goal that the behavior of the young women not lead to the word of God being maligned. Yet there is not enough information present in the context of the passage to decide the matter. The fact that an exhortation regarding appropriate behavior is prompted by occasional circumstances does not imply that the exhortation would no longer apply in other contexts. Grounds for the culture-bound or transcultural nature of the wife's submission to her husband must be found elsewhere in Scripture. If you look at other places in Paul's writings (Ephesians 5:22 and Colossians 3:18), he clearly states that the wife is to be willingly subject to her husband. Plus, Peter clearly states the same idea in 1 Peter 3:1. It is best in this case to let the clear meaning of Scripture inform the unclear meaning.

For (2), the urgency with which Paul instructs Titus to get on with the unfinished business of appointing elders would indicate his belief that the need for shepherding in Crete is pressing. This could reflect that inappropriate behavior among the younger (and possibly older) women was already occurring in Crete, and Paul was reacting to that situation. Bruce Winter's work[80] on the possible influence of the new Roman woman upon Cretan society and making its way into the church can be helpful here, although as we've stated above, there is no direct evidence that the phenomenon of the new Roman woman had any influence upon Cretan society.

The passage Titus 2:3–5 occurs within the broader section Titus 2:2–10, in which Paul is exhorting Titus to teach the older men, older women (who in turn will instruct the younger women), younger men, and slaves to conduct their lives in a way that makes the gospel attractive, and will not cause the word of God to be maligned. This is a form of "household code" for the church in Crete. Titus is to teach the older women to be holy, not slanderers or given to much wine, but teachers of the good. By living such lives, worthy of respect, they will be able

---

80. See Winter, *Roman Wives, Roman Widows,* 141–169.

to train the younger women to love their husbands and children, to be self-controlled and pure, and to be good homemakers and subject to their husbands. Such behavior by both the older and younger women would be culturally desirable, so the word of God would not be maligned, but it is unclear whether a younger woman's desirable characteristic of subjection to her husband is tied to the culture of first-century Crete or transcends that culture and is still applicable today. The resolution of this issue requires a broader consideration of what Scripture teaches on the roles of women and men within the marriage covenant, and the obligations of spouses to one another within that covenant. For a good review of that broader consideration of Scripture, see the papers on the household codes of Colossians 3:18–19, Ephesians 5:21–33, and 1 Peter 3:1–7 in this collection of papers on "The Bible and Gender."

Reflections

1. Older women are to teach younger women with a focus on spiritual formation.

2. Women share their experience and spirituality in the teaching ministry.

3. Women with experience as wives are to instruct other women regarding marriage.

4. Women with experience as mothers are to instruct other women regarding parenting.

5. Women are to teach other women how to overcome sin and remain pure.

6. Women are to teach other women how to become self-controlled.

7. Christian women are to live virtuous lives and avoid dishonoring the church.

Bibliography

Banker, John. *A Semantic and Structural Analysis of Titus*. Dallas TX: Summer Institute of Linguistics, 1987.

Greenlee, J. Harold. *An Exegetical Summary of Titus & Philemon*. Second Edition. Dallas, TX: Summer Institute of Linguistics, 2008.

Knight, George W. *The Pastoral Epistles*. The New International Greek Testament Commentary. Grand Rapids, MI: Eerdmans, 1992.

Levinsohn, Stephen H. "The Relevance of Greek Discourse Studies to Exegesis." *Journal of Translation* 2(2) (2006): 11–21.

Marshall, I. Howard. *The Pastoral Epistles*. The International Critical Commentary. London, UK: T&T Clark, 1999.

Mounce, William D. *Pastoral Epistles*. Word Biblical Commentary Volume 46. Grand Rapids, MI: Zondervan, 2000.

Payne, Philip B. *Man and Woman, One in Christ: An Exegetical and Theological Study of Paul's Letters*. Grand Rapids, MI: Zondervan, 2009.

Perkins, Larry J. *The Pastoral Letters: A Handbook on the Greek Text*. *Baylor Handbook on the Greek New Testament*. Waco, TX: Baylor University Press, 2017.

Runge, Steven E. *Discourse Grammar of New Testament Greek*. Peabody, MA: Hendrickson, 2010.

Towner, Philip H. *The Letters to Timothy and Titus*. The New International Commentary on the New Testament. Grand Rapids, MI: Eerdmans, 2006.

Winter, Bruce W. *Roman Wives, Roman Widows: The Appearance of New Women and the Pauline Communities*. Grand Rapids, MI: Eerdmans, 2003.

Witherington, Ben. *A Socio-Rhetorical Commentary on Titus, 1-2 Timothy and 1-3 John, Letters and Homilies for Hellenized Christians,* Volume 1. Downers Grove, IL: InterVarsity Press, 2006.

Yarbrough, Robert W. *The Letters to Timothy and Titus.* The Pillar New Testament Commentary. Ed. D.A. Carson. Grand Rapids, MI: Eerdmans, 2018.

CHAPTER EIGHT

1 Peter 3:1–7

Kay S. McKean, Joey Harris,
and Steve Kinnard

Abstract

Having considered the household codes of Paul found in Colossians 3 and Ephesians 5–6, this paper focuses on the household code of the Apostle Peter in 1 Peter 3:1–7. The reader should view the three household codes side by side and discern the similarities and differences in the codes. If you have not read the paper on Colossians 3 and Ephesians 5 in this collection, then it is advisable to do so. It serves as a good introduction to Peter's household code.

Introduction

The apostle Peter's first letter was written in approximately AD 65 and addressed to "God's elect" in the world. The new Christian religion, with Judaism as its roots, was facing its first trials of widespread persecution. Although the Jewish religion was a *religio licita* (a legitimate and permitted religion under the Roman government), the new Christian faith had come under suspicion because of its teachings of a risen Messiah and also due to misunderstandings of their belief in a new "Kingdom." Initially, Christianity was considered a sect of Judaism and enjoyed the benefits of its legal status. However, in time, Christianity became viewed as a separate sect, and lost the legal privileges of Judaism. The Christians were not enjoying the legal status that the apostle Paul had when he avoided scourging by claiming his Roman citizenship (Acts 22:25–29).

Although the authorship of 1 Peter has been questioned, it is widely accepted that Peter is the writer of this letter. There is a hint that the letter may have been edited by Silvanus (1 Peter 5:12), acting as Peter's *amanuensis*, and perhaps bringing Peter's writing style up to higher standards than Peter's capabilities would have allowed.

If the correct dating of the letter is the mid-60s AD, then this letter follows the beginnings of the intense persecution instigated by the

Roman Emperor Nero in AD 64. Peter realized that the situation for Christians was only getting worse, and the theme throughout his letter was to prepare them for the suffering that was to come. His goal was to admonish them to remain faithful in difficult times and to live lives that would be respectful and pleasing to God, even in the midst of "all kinds of trials" (1 Peter 1:6). Of utmost importance was the reminder to live as light in a dark and hostile world (1 Peter 2:9) and to remember Jesus who had suffered for them (1 Peter 2:21).

The letter was presumably to be circulated to those who had been scattered by persecution and were living in the region now known as Turkey, but which in the first century was identified as Pontus, Galatia, Cappadocia, Asia, and Bithynia (1 Peter 1:2).

There were several examples in the letter of what it meant to live "good lives among the pagans" (1 Peter 2:12), but one of the identifying marks of the Christian was the use of the word "submission." Peter uses this word in his household code in chapter 3. Peter spoke of submission to governing authorities, slaves in submission to masters, wives in submission to husbands, and young men in submission to those who are older. Each of these calls to submission was not for the sake of submission alone; they each had a purpose. That purpose was ultimately that their behavior would bring about God's purpose in their lives and in the lives of those around them. The example for submission was found in the person of Jesus Christ, who entrusted himself to God in life and in death (1 Peter 2:23).

Submission was not a rule to be obeyed, but was rather an attitude and a lifestyle.

This was quite a radical idea in the first century. After all, since the Roman Empire was a tyrannical regime, wives, slaves, and young people had few rights, so submission was a frightening idea. The idea of voluntarily submitting one's will to another was radical. But again and again in his household code Peter expects submission because it indicates submission toward God.

The passage of our focus is found in 1 Peter 3:1–7. In calling all Christians to a lifestyle that reflects the heart of Jesus, Peter narrows his field to speak directly to a certain group of women. In doing this, he gives us the example of women heroes in the faith and brings forth a pattern that will be applicable to all.

Wives

1 Peter 3:1–6 (NIV2011)

¹Wives, in the same way submit yourselves to your own husbands so that, if any of them do not believe the word, they may be won over without words by the behavior of their wives, ²when they see the purity and reverence of your lives. ³Your beauty should not come from outward adornment, such as elaborate hairstyles and the wearing of gold jewelry or fine clothes. ⁴Rather, it should be that of your inner self, the unfading beauty of a gentle and quiet spirit, which is of great worth in God's sight. ⁵For this is the way the holy women of the past who put their hope in God used to adorn themselves. They submitted themselves to their own husbands, ⁶like Sarah, who obeyed Abraham and called him her lord. You are her daughters if you do what is right and do not give way to fear.

Exegesis

The word ὁμοίως, *homoiōs* ("in the same way, similarly") is used to bring the concepts relating to submission together with various groups of people. Each act of submission was to guide the thoughts of the Christians back to the heart and actions of Jesus. Peter's letter includes the women who may have been hesitant to follow the example of submission. We can speculate that Christian wives may have been questioning their need to submit to a man who was not a follower of Christ. Peter's instructions also contrast with what might have been a tendency to want to separate from an unbelieving partner, especially during this time of impending crisis. He agrees with Paul's letters to the Corinthians on this matter: "And if a woman has a husband who is not a believer and he is willing to live with her, she must not divorce him" (1 Corinthians 7:13).

In 1 Peter 3:1, "wives submit yourselves" ὑποτασσόμεναι (*hypotassomenai,* from the verb ὑποτάσσω, hypotássō, "to cause to be in a submissive relationship, to subject, to subordinate" [BDAG]) was to adopt a posture that would ultimately lead to winning a person over. ὑποτασσόμεναι (*hypotassomenai*) is a present middle or passive participle, and the middle voice stresses the emphasis that it is the subject that willingly or voluntarily submits. The present tense often conveys continual action (though not always). Thus, the phrase could be translated as "Wives, you continue to submit yourselves to your own husbands."

Considering the Roman law that asserted a husband's absolute authority over his wife, it was important for a Christian wife to find her way in living out her faith without alienating her husband, especially if he was not a follower of Christ. While it may have been understandable and acceptable in that time and culture for a woman with a believing husband to submit herself to him, wives with unbelieving husbands might have considered assuming a different posture. Equally important to note is that while we cannot say for certain the exact circumstances of the women who were recipients of Peter's letter, we can assume that many of the Christian wives came from Jewish backgrounds. Their Jewish husbands would look upon the Christian faith as a "false teaching," which would bring about even more stress in the marriage relationship and the temptation to pull away from their husbands in order to keep their faith. This contrasts with what Peter is teaching these women, as he reassures them that they can have a submissive spirit without fear. He goes on to say that the way to win over their husbands was not to apply more outward beauty but to develop the inner beauty of a Christlike spirit.

For a wife to submit to a husband, whether he is a believer or an unbeliever, is a voluntary decision about how she will relate to him. Just as Jesus placed himself within the will of God, wives who entrust themselves to God can have confidence the Father will guide and protect them in their marriage relationship. Submission is not a self-denigrating act but one that allows God to work.

It is interesting that after directing the wives to be submissive, Peter writes that they should embrace a different kind of beauty than the world expects. Peter says to be adorned with purity, reverence, gentleness, and quietness. We will discuss those words in more detail, but first it is helpful to look at the word "adornment." In verse three, Peter instructs the women not to be adorned in a "worldly" fashion, using the word that also describes the orderly fashion of the world (κόσμος – *kosmos*). Later in verse five, he uses a similar word (ἐκόσμουν – *ekosmoun*) that means, "to put in order so as to appear neat or well organized, make *neat/tidy*"(BDAG). (This is where we get our word "cosmetic.") The message to Christian wives centers on how they were to "arrange" their countenance. Outward accessories such as elaborate hair styles, gold jewelry, and expensive clothes were not the defining mark of a beautiful woman from God's viewpoint. The world around them would find these things valuable, but God finds value in the "hidden person of the heart" or the "inner self" (v. 4). These qualities are not immediately seen by anyone but God, although they are displayed in interactions with others. Time, effort, and expense is wasted on "arranging" the outward qualities that fade, but God has his good promises in store for those who "arrange" their attitude and even their personality around what is precious to him.

Peter's use of the example of Sarah is an interesting one.[81] Abraham was a man who several times put his wife in awkward and dangerous situations (Genesis 12, 20). And Sarah had her own faults: She was demanding, manipulative, and at times cruel. She sent her handmaiden to a likely death along with the handmaiden's young son. (If God had not intervened, they could have died [Genesis 21:10]). She blamed God and her husband for her problems (Genesis 16:2, 5). When given the promise of a child, she laughed and later lied (Genesis 18:15). The only time that the Scriptures record her calling Abraham her "lord" occurs when she was amazed and baffled by what she overheard concerning the birth of Isaac (Genesis 18:12).[82]

Sarah was not faultless. However, Peter reminds his readers that Sarah, like the first-century women who would hear Peter's words, was a recipient of a promise. She was the one chosen to give birth to Abraham's child. Abraham would not be the Father of the Faith without Sarah becoming the Mother of the Faith. Peter claims that if the women who believe in Jesus do what is right and do not give way to fear, they too will receive the promise of God—not a baby but salvation.

Despite Sarah's errors that are recorded in Scripture, Peter's letter affirms the fact that she was known by people of faith as a good wife to Abraham who stayed by him through thick and thin, traveling to distant lands and being exposed to a challenging way of life. In using

---

81. Sly, D. I. "1 Peter 3:6b in the Light of Philo and Josephus." *Journal of Biblical Literature* 110 (1991): 126—129.

82. "The Testament of Abraham," a Greek narrative written in the first century AD and possibly available in Peter's lifetime, chronicles an interaction between Sarah and Abraham, with her affectionately calling him "lord" (Greek – *kurios* – sir, master, lord) several times.

her as an example, Peter is reminding the women that the challenges they encounter in their marriage can be faced with confidence that God will intervene, as he did with Sarah when Abraham made choices that were not entirely best for her. For example, on two occasions Abraham sent his wife to live in a king's harem to secure his own safety. But in both instances Sarah's identity as Abraham's wife was revealed, and they were sent away without harm and in fact with an abundance of gifts (Genesis 12, 20). Of course, she is best known as the mother who gave birth in her old age and is recognized as a hero in the eyes of her physical and spiritual descendants. We see how beloved she was by Abraham in the way Abraham honored her following her death. Abraham's loyalty to her in securing her burial spot takes a full chapter in our modern Bibles (Genesis 23).

Peter also uses examples of the "holy women of the past." Their "adornment" was the point of Peter's exhortation. The Old Testament Scriptures portray many women of faith, and ironically, most of them, in moments of crisis, were not acting in subordination to a husband. For example: Deborah, Jael, Abigail, Hannah, the Shunammite woman, and even Esther were in positions of taking charge of situations without consulting their husbands on the matter. However, each of these women had, in the end, her husband's best interest in mind. They had adorned themselves with courage and faith when the circumstances called for them. Again, we do not have recorded for us all the examples of the holy women that Peter is referring to, but we can assume that by his pointing to women of the past, the recipients of his letter would understand his intent.

The qualities that Peter emphasizes are those of purity, reverence, gentleness, and quietness. These are unfading qualities that God looks for in women of faith, in every age of history and every culture.

1. When a husband of a Christian wife viewed her **purity** (ἀγνὴν, *hagnēn*), he would be confident in her faithfulness to the marriage relationship. A Christian wife would not have any hint of sexual impropriety, and this purity would give the husband security and respect for her and for her new religion. This was important in a day and age when women might be lured into cults that encouraged sexual promiscuity.

2. **Reverence, fear, reverent fear** (φόβῳ, *phobō*) for God would be obvious. The Christian wife would not be able to conceal her devotion to God, evidenced by prayer and obedience to her faith.

3. The Christian wife would develop a **gentle** character, following that quality in Jesus. The word πραέως (*praeōs*) describes someone who is humble, considerate, compassionate, and tender. It is the opposite of rough, loud, or harsh. Again, the husband would be attracted to being treated in a gentle manner, especially if these qualities were not the norm for the wife before she became a Christian.

4. The word **"quiet"** is sometimes misunderstood to refer to silence. Obviously in context Peter is making the point that the woman will "win over" her husband without a word. However, the implication is not on the fact that she will never utter a sound, but that the most powerful and emphatic message that her husband is receiving is from the demeanor that she is displaying. "Quiet" (ἡσυχίος, *hēsychios*) means literally to "keep one's seat." It can also be translated as "well ordered" (BDAG). It implies an attitude that is undisturbed, still, and calm. Paul used the word *hēsychios* in writing to the Thessalonians: "Make it your ambition to lead a *quiet* life…so that your daily life may win the respect of outsiders" (1 Thessalonians 4:11–12, emphasis added). Again, the motive is to help others to see God's work in the life of the Christian. A Christian wife will not be restless, nervous, or exhibit an overanxious perspective, because she trusts in God.

After instructing the wives on holy living, Peter switches his focus to the husbands.

Husbands

1 Peter 3:7, NIV2011

Husbands, in the same way be considerate as you live with your wives, and treat them with respect as the weaker partner and as heirs with you of the gracious gift of life, so that nothing will hinder your prayers.

Christian husbands are called to give honor (τιμήν, *timēn,* "value, esteem, dignity") to their wives. Giving honor to another person implies that you are lifting them up with value. Although the wife's duty of submission might imply an over/under relationship, it is countered with the duty of the husband to highly esteem and give dignity to his wife. Thus, we can see that the point in Peter's letter is not simply the arrangement of roles, but respect for the other person and self-sacrifice. The Christlike attributes outlined in this passage lead to a marriage that brings glory to God and blissful satisfaction to a husband and wife.

Furthermore, Peter reminds the husbands that their wives are coheirs with them. In a patriarchal world, the very idea of spiritual equality had to be emphasized. Although Peter claims that women are the "weaker vessel," this only implies weaker physically; and it is a generalization. It is a generally true statement that females are not as muscularly strong as men.[83] The contrast between a man and a woman biologically is used to point out that their physical differences do not reflect an inferiority in their spiritual capacity. In fact, the physical "weakness" underscores even more the need for the husband to behave in a way that is respectful and caring, particularly in an era when the vulnerability of women left them little recourse for protection. Any interpretation that implies that women are weaker spiritually does not concur with Peter's assertion that women are coheirs (συγκληρονόμος, *synklēronómos,* literally "inheriting together with") with their husbands.

The passage in Peter's letter corresponds to the letters from Paul to the churches in Ephesus and Colossae, where wives are also called to submit to their husbands, and husbands are called to love and care for their wives (Ephesians 5; Colossians 3). With what we know about the cultural norms of the people who first read these letters, the reminders to the women were probably quite consistent with the expectations of their first-century world. What may have been unique and even stunning was the emphasis placed on how the husbands should treat their wives. Marriage was no longer to be seen as one partner dominating another, but each one doing whatever could be done to meet the other's needs.

As we look at the instructions given regarding marriage, it is improbable that Peter's or Paul's concern had to do with ensuring which

---

83. *Recovering Biblical Manhood and Womanhood,* by John Piper and Wayne Grudem. "The Biological Basis for Gender Specific Behavior" Gregg Johnson, 1991

partner was "the boss." Unfortunately, that seems to be the overriding focus in our modern studies that deal with this subject. The emphasis on roles has, in many ways, usurped what the authors originally were trying to convey. Marriage, as a microcosm of the church, provides the opportunity for two people to "grow up into him who is the Head, that is Christ…as each part does its work" (Ephesians 4:15–16). Marriage is a duet, a dance, in which the two partners create something that they could not create without each other. The goal, as always, was that a Christlike spirit would be displayed in the lives of men and women who were called out of darkness into light.

But what about the wives whose husbands don't want to join in the dance? As many modern-day women find themselves in that situation, the answer from Peter remains the same: A wife must never compromise her purity and obedience to God, but she can trust in God as she carries a Christlike demeanor toward her husband. Resistance would only occur when her standards of righteousness might be compromised. The strength required when a wife is the only partner exercising this kind of attitude is immense and should be highly respected by people of faith.

One final note to remember is that Peter's marital status is specifically mentioned in Matthew 8:14, when Jesus entered Peter's house. Peter's mother-in-law was sick with a fever, and Jesus healed her. Although Peter's wife is not placed in this picture, having a mother-in-law can only mean that Peter was married. Also, in a letter written to the Corinthian church, the apostle Paul argues that he had a right to bring along a believing wife, as "Cephas" (Peter's Greek name) did[84] (1 Corinthians 9:5). The reason this is important is that Peter, in contrast to other New Testament writers, is directing his readers to a way of relating to one another in marriage that he most likely had to learn and understand himself. Our impression of Peter as an insensitive and impulsive fisherman is tempered by the fact that he alone was willing to listen to the women who came to proclaim the resurrection of Jesus: "But they did not believe the women, because their words seemed to them like nonsense. Peter, however, got up and ran to the tomb" (Luke 24:11–12, emphasis added). As the author of this letter to Christians learning a new way of life, Peter's response to the women exemplifies the very attitude and heart that he espouses: one of humility, submissiveness, and respect.

---

84. Paul's argument was hypothetical; at that time, he was unmarried.

Bibliography

BDAG. William Arndt, Frederick W. Danker, and Walter Bauer, *A Greek-English Lexicon of the New Testament and Other Early Christian Literature* (Chicago: University of Chicago Press, 2000).

Gandry, Stanley, James Beck, ed. *Two Views on Women in Ministry.* Grand Rapids, Michigan: Zondervan, 2001.

James, Carolyn Custis. *When Life and Beliefs Collide.* Grand Rapids, Michigan: Zondervan, 2001.

Keener, Craig. *Paul, Women and Wives.* Peabody, Massachusetts: Hendrickson Publishers, Inc., 1992.

The New International Version (Grand Rapids, MI: Zondervan, 2011).

Pierce, Ronald W., and Rebecca Merrill Groothuis. *Discovering Biblical Equality.* Downers Grove, Illinois: InterVarsity Press, 2005.

Piper, John, Wayne Grudem, ed. *Recovering Biblical Manhood and Womanhood,* Wheaton, Illinois: Crossway, 1991.

Tenney, Merrill. *New Testament Survey, Revised,* Grand Rapids, Michigan: Wm B. Eerdmans Publishing Company, 1985.

Winter, Bruce W. *Roman Wives, Roman Widows.* Grand Rapids, Michigan: Wm B. Eerdmans Publishing Company, 2003.

AUTHORS

Dr. Glenn W. Giles has served in a teaching capacity in the Denver Church of Christ for 29 years. He was appointed Teacher in 2000 and Elder in 2008. Dr. Giles completed his B.S. Degree in Physical Science from Colorado State University, his M.Div. in New Testament from Lincoln Christian University, his Th.M. in New Testament from Trinity Evangelical Divinity School, and his Ph.D. in Biblical Studies from Trinity Theological Seminary. He also completed his Ph.D. residency in Religious Studies at Marquette University and his B.S. in Pharmacy from the University of Colorado. He is a Registered Pharmacist as well as the Founder, Director, and Professor of Bible and Theology at Rocky Mountain School of Ministry and Theology in Denver, Colorado. He is also an Adjunct Professor of Bible at Lincoln Christian University. His specialties are in Soteriology, Eschatology, Hermeneutics, Acts, and the Sermon on the Mount. His Doctoral Thesis was on Matthew 7:21-23 and his Th.M. Thesis was on Matthew 21:43. Glenn and his wife Linda have been married for 46 years and have 3 great children (and spouses) and four amazing grandchildren. Glenn and Linda love to vacation on their ranch in the beautiful mountains of Colorado.

Joseph Harris is an author, teacher and speaker specializing in helping people to understand the Bible and to experience deeper love by living according to the teachings of Jesus. He has a degree in Molecular Biology from Princeton University, a Masters in Adult Education from the University of Phoenix, and has done graduate study in Education at Montclair State University, in Dynamics of Organization at the University of Pennsylvania and biblical languages at the University of a Pennsylvania and the Rocky Mountain School of Ministry and Theology and post-graduate religious studies at Columbia Biblical Seminary, Princeton Theological Seminary and Trinity Theological Seminary. Joey and his wife, Debbie, have three children in college. Joey has an international teaching and speaking ministry called Teach Me the Bible. He is also the co-director and a founding teacher of the Athens Institute of Ministry (www.athensinstitute.org), which teaches courses in biblical and religious studies online and in various locations internationally.

Dr. G. Steve Kinnard has served as a Teacher/Evangelist with the New York City Church of Christ for 36 years. He is currently co-chair of the ICOC Teachers Service Team. Steve completed his B.A. in Bible and

Literature from Freed-Hardeman College, his M.Div. with Languages from Southeastern Baptist Theological Seminary, and his D.Min. from Drew University. Steve is an Adjunct Professor of Bible at Lincoln Christian University. He is also Professor of Bible and Dean of the Bible Department at the Rocky Mountain School of Ministry and Theology. Steve has authored twenty books including *King Jesus, The Way of the Heart,* and *Jesus Unequaled.* In the summer of 2020, he is publishing a new translation of the Greek New Testament entitled *The King Jesus Translation* (KJT). Steve and his wife Leigh have been married for 38 years. They have two children, Chelsea married to Rob Novack and Daniel married to Corrine, and they have two energetic and loving grandsons, Bradley and Tyler (T-Ty). Steve loves classic rock, novels, and football.

Valdur Koha serves as an Elder and Teacher in the Boston Church of Christ. He also serves as the president of the European Missions Society and the executive chairman of the Beam Missions Foundation which funds leadership training programs around the world. Valdur is a member of the ICOC Teacher's Service Team. Born in Germany in 1955, Valdur lives with his family in Boston since 1985. Valdur and Irene are married since 1980; they have five sons and one daughter (all disciples) and six grandchildren.

Suzette Lewis is a Women's Ministry Leader and is part of the Co-Leadership team of the Toronto Church of Christ with her husband Andrew. She graduated from Brock University in Adult Education and later completed a master's degree in Conflict Analysis and Management at Royal Roads University, in Victoria B.C. Suzette became a disciple in 1989 as a single parent. Married for 28 years, she has 2 adult children and 3 grandchildren. She fell in love with her community upon joining a counselling and advocacy team in the field of violence against women, and later went on to teach Justice Studies as a college professor. Suzette is a qualified Mediator and Trainer of Restorative Practices and Victim Offender Reconciliation. Building on that passion for her community, she is President of Make Your Mark, a Youth Leadership Enterprise that empowers young girls for change and societal influence. As the Executive Director of the Murray McKinnon Foundation, Suzette is responsible for the overall strategic direction and operation of programs including Youth in Conflict with the Law. Her diverse experiences with women and families have given her a deep appreciation for how people can improve the quality of their lives one step at a time.

Dr. Gregg Marutzky is the Senior Minister for the Antelope Valley Church of Christ in Lancaster, California. Gregg and Cathy have been married for 39 years having met in high school. Gregg became a Christian at the University of Colorado and graduated with a B.S. in Civil Engineering and a B.S. in Business Administration. Gregg worked as a civil engineer before he entered fulltime ministry. He continued his education at Pepperdine University receiving a M.S. in Ministry and a Master of Divinity. Gregg later gained a Doctor of Ministry degree from Abilene Christian University and M.S. in Clinical Counseling from the University of Nebraska. Gregg is currently pursuing a PhD in Leadership from Johnson University. Gregg is the Dean of the Los Angeles School of Ministry plus teaches at the Rocky Mountain School of Theology and Ministry. He also guest lectures at Rochester University. Gregg is a national board certified counselor and a Licensed Marriage and Family Therapist in California. Gregg has been in the ministry for 38 years leading churches in Denver, Dallas, Omaha, Los Angeles and San Diego. He has also served in campus ministry at UCLA, San Diego State, MIT, University of Colorado, Long Beach State University, University of Nebraska, and SMU. Gregg and Cathy have two daughters, Amanda married to Kyle living in Orange County, California and Megan married to Chad plus three grandchildren (Sienna, Makenna, and Dean) living in Dallas, Texas.

Kay Summers McKean was raised in Miami and graduated from the University of Florida in 1975. She and her husband Randy have served in ministries in South Carolina, Florida, Massachusetts, Japan, and throughout Europe. She most recently served as the director for Women's Ministries with the Northern Virginia Church of Christ, just outside of Washington D.C. Kay is an author of several books, including *In The Beginning, Love Your Husband* (coauthored with Gloria Baird), *A Women's Ministry Handbook* (coauthored with Jennifer Lambert), and *Radical Love* (coauthored with her husband Randy McKean). In June of 2012, Kay was invited to be one of the first women to serve on the Teachers' Service Team of the International Churches of Christ. This step has led to more inclusion of the female voice in various arenas of church leadership. Kay considers one of her greatest ministry accomplishments to be ensuring that the women's perspective on church matters is heard. Although now retired, she strives to be a lifelong learner and advocate for women in the church.

Dr. Rolan Monje serves as an evangelist, teacher, and author. He is director of the Asia-Pacific Leadership Academy in Manila and professor of Hebrew and Old Testament at Rocky Mountain School of Ministry and Theology in Colorado. Rolan graduated with honors from both University of the Philippines (BS Electrical Engineering) and University of London (Bachelor of Divinity, emphasis in biblical languages). He earned his masters and doctorate (MMin Historical Theology; DMin in Pastoral Theology) from American Bible College, Florida. Dr. Monje has written five commentary books on the Old Testament including his most recent, *Remember the Lord: Reflections on the Book of Dueteronomy.* Rolan heads an international teaching ministry that has taken him to some forty countries across six continents. He and his wife, Weng, make their home in Manila with their two daughters, Yana and Stefi, and a mini-schnauzer named Razu.

Dr. Brian W. Perkins has served as the Lead Evangelist of the Louisville Church of Christ for 11 years with his wife Shann. He serves as a Teacher for the ACR family of churches. He completed his Masters in Electrical Engineering at the University of Michigan, and his Ph.D. in Comprehensive Theology from Trinity Theological Seminary. Brian and Shann have been married for 24 years and have two faithful children, Wynstin and Whitney, who are in the Teen ministry.

Jeanie Shaw has served in the ministry for forty-six years. For eight of those years, she also served as a Vice-President for *HOPE worldwide.* She has taught classes and workshops on various topics around the world and has authored fifteen books. Jeanie completed her B.S. from the University of Florida and recently received her Masters' degree in Spiritual Formation from Regent University. She is pursuing her doctorate in the same field. Jeanie was married for forty-five years to Wyndham, who recently transitioned to Paradise. Jeanie has four adult children, eight grandchildren, and a golden retriever, all of whom bring her great joy.

Dr. Scott Warlow has served as a Teacher with the Toronto Church of Christ since November of 2018. He was baptized in 1992 while completing his Ph.D. in Mathematical Physics at the University of Toronto. After being awarded an ABD in Finance from the Schulich School of Business in 2002, he has worked in the Asset Management industry for the past 18 years. He holds an Intermediate Certificate in Scientific Apologetics from Reasons to Believe, and has been a volunteer apologist with RTB since 2013, and was recently asked to join their visiting scholar program. He is currently completing his M.Div., specializing in Biblical Studies, at Tyndale Seminary in Toronto. Scott and his wife Marion have been married for 22 years and have led groups in the campus, singles and marrieds ministries. They have two wonderful teenage daughters, both disciples of Christ. Scott loves golf, travel, and reading.